The Childcare Act 2006

Fergus Smith

B.Sc.(Hons), M.A., C.Q.S.W., D.M.S., Dip.M

D1382549

Children Act Enterprises Ltd (CAE)
103 Mayfield Road
South Croydon
Surrey CR2 0BH

www.caeuk.org

© Fergus Smith 2007

British Library Cataloguing in Publication Data
A catalogue record for this book is available from the
British Library

ISBN 978-1-899986-47-7

Designed and typeset by Andrew Haig & Associates
Printed in the UK by The Lavenham Press

CAE is an independent organisation which publishes
guides to family and criminal law and provides
consultancy, research, training and independent
investigation services to the public, private and voluntary
sectors.

Contents

Introduction   1
Key Points   2
Definitions   3

Part 1 – General Functions of Local Authority: England

Improvements of Young Children's Well Being   9
Provision of Childcare   15
Information, Advice & Assistance   24
Miscellaneous   33

Part 2 – General Functions of Local Authority: Wales

Provision of Childcare   37
Information, Advice & Assistance   41
Miscellaneous   43

Part 3 – Regulation of Provision of Childcare in England

General Functions of Chief Inspector   47

Regulation of Early Years Provision

Requirements to Register   50
Process of Registration   54
Requirements to be Met by Early Years Providers   59
Inspection   67

Regulation of Later Years Provision

Requirements to Register   70
Process of Registration   74

Regulation 79
Inspection 82

Voluntary Registration
Process of Voluntary Registration 84
Regulation of Persons Registering Voluntarily 90

Common Provisions
Cancellation of Registration etc 93
Cancellation in an Emergency 98
Registration – Procedural Safeguards 100
Disqualification from Registration 104
Rights of Entry 110
Reports & Information 114
Offences & Criminal Proceedings 118
Miscellaneous & Interpretation 121

Part 4 – Miscellaneous & General
Provision of Information About Children –
England & Wales 129

Appendices
1: Implementation Schedule 132
2: Source Material 134
3: CAE Publications 135

Introduction

- This guide provides easy access to an accurate summary of the Childcare Act 2006 which was passed in order to implement recommendations and priorities set out in:

  - (In England) *'Choice for parents – the best start for children: a ten year strategy for childcare –* HM Treasury 2004
  - (In Wales) *Childcare is for Children* 2005

- The Act removes the current legal distinction between childcare and education in the early years to better reflect how young children learn and develop and also introduces a new regulation and inspection system which creates (for England , with effect from September 2008) an:

  - 'Early Years Register' for childcare of those aged 0 to 5 (where a key requirement will be delivery of the Early Years Foundation Stage (EYFS) and
  - 'Ofsted Childcare Register' (OCR) for those providing for older children as well as those catering for the younger age group but not required to be registered on the Early Years Register

- This edition reflects available **draft** regulations and statutory guidance.

  NB. Appendix 1 provides an implementation schedule of dates on which sections of the Act came into/are believed to be coming into force.

Key Points

- The Act requires local authorities in England and [with the exception of the 1st objective] Wales, to:

  - Improve 'well-being' (defined by the 5 outcome of 'Every Child Matters' as staying safe, being healthy, enjoying and achieving, making a positive contribution and achieving economic well being)
  - Secure sufficient child care for working parents and those making the transition to work, including some 'free to charge' provision, and to regularly assess demand
  - Provide an information service for parents and children on services, facilities and publications that might assist them

- The Act gives the government power to:

  - Integrate and review regulation and inspection of early education and child care
  - Create a single framework of learning and development from birth to 5 (the 'Early Years Foundation Stage' EYFS)
  - Require local authorities to encourage involvement of parents and private providers in the establishment of integrated early years services

Definitions

- For the purposes of Part 1 (general functions of local authority in England) and Part 3 (regulation of childcare provision in England), the following definitions apply.

Childcare [s.18]

- 'Childcare' means any form of care for a child and, (subject to s.18(3)) care includes:

  - Education for a child, and
  - Any other supervised activity for a child [s.18(2)]

- Childcare does **not** include:

  - Education (or any other supervised activity) provided by a school during school hours for a registered pupil who is not a 'young child', or
  - Any form of health care for a child [s.18(3)]

- Childcare does **not** include care provided by a:

  - Parent or step-parent of the child
  - Person with parental responsibility for the child
  - Relative of the child
  - Local authority foster parent to the child
  - Person who is a foster parent with whom the child has been placed by a voluntary organisation
  - Person who fosters the child privately [s.18(4)]

- Childcare does **not** include care provided for a child if the care is provided:

- In any of the following establishments as part of its activities – an appropriate children's home, a care home, a hospital in which the child is a patient, a residential family centre and
- By the person carrying on the establishment or a person employed to work at the establishment [s.18(5)]

NB. Reference above to a person who is 'employed' includes a reference to a person who is employed under a contract for service [s.18 (6)].

■ Childcare does **not** include care provided for a child who is detained in a young offender institution (YOI), or in a secure training centre (STC) [s.18 (7)].

NB. In s.18, appropriate children's home, local authority foster parent, to foster a child privately and voluntary organisation have the same meaning as in the Children Act 1989; care home, hospital and residential family centre have the same meaning as in the Care Standards Act 2000 and relative, in relation to a child, means a grandparent, aunt, uncle brother or sister, whether of the full blood or half blood or by marriage or civil partnership [s.18(8)].

Early Years Provision [s.20 & s.96]

■ 'Early years provision' means the provision of childcare for a 'young child' (see below for definition) and an early years provider is a person who provides early years provision.

■ 'Early years childminding' means early years provision on domestic premises for reward and early years childminder should be read accordingly.

*NB. Early years provision on domestic premises for reward is **not** early years childminding **if** at any time, the number of persons providing or assisting with the provision on the premises exceeds 3 [s.96(5)].*

Later Years Provision [s.96 (7) – (9)]

■ 'Later years provision' means the provision of childcare for a child older than a 'young child' as defined below.

■ 'Later years childminding' means later years provision on domestic premises for reward and later years childminding should be read accordingly.

NB. Later years provision on domestic premises for reward is not 'later years childminding if at any time, the number of persons providing or assisting with the provision on the premises exceeds 3 [s.96(9)].

Young Child [s.19]

■ A child is a 'young child' during the period:

  • Beginning with her/his birth to
  • Ending immediately before the 1st September next following the date on which s/he attains the age of 5 [s.19]

Part 1: General Functions of Local Authority – England

Improvement of Young Children's Well-Being

General Duties of Local Authority in Relation to Well-Being of Young Children [s.1]

■ An English local authority must:

  • Improve the well-being of young children in its area, and
  • Reduce inequalities between young children in its area in relation to their 'well-being' [s.1(1)]

  NB. 'Well-being' in this Act means children's physical and mental health and emotional well-being, protection from harm and neglect, education, training and recreation, contribution made by them to society and their social and economic well-being [s.1(2)]

■ The Secretary of State may, via regulations [see below], set targets for the above and in exercising their functions, an English local authority must act in the manner best calculated to secure that any such targets are met [s.1(3);(4)].

■ In performing its s.1 duties, an English local authority must also have regard to any guidance given from time to time by the Secretary of State [s.1(5)].

■ See below for the **draft** version of the above mentioned regulations the consultation period for which ended on 31st January 2007.

The [draft] Childcare Act (Local Authority Targets) Regulations 2007

■ The Secretary of State must set targets (as per s.1 (3) above) no more frequently than once a year [reg.3].

■ Targets must relate to children's development as measured by the assessment scales of the 'Foundation Stage Profile' [reg.4]

■ Prior to setting targets, the Secretary of State must inform the local authority:

- That s/he is proposing to set targets
- Of any deadline (at least a month after notification) for representations or proposals to be made by her/him
- Of the date (at least 2 months after notification)by which s/he proposes to finalise the targets [reg.5]

■ If they are made prior to the deadline, the Secretary of State must take into account any:

- Targets proposed by the local authority
- Representations made by the local authority and
- Representations made by relevant partners (defined as in s.4 of the Act) [reg.6]

■ If the Secretary of State proposes to set targets that differ from any which have been proposed by the local authority prior the deadline, s/he must:

- Give the local authority an account of her/his reasons

- Allow the local authority at least 1 month to make further representations and
- When appropriate, inform the local authority of a revised date on s/he proposes to finalise the targets [reg.7]

Meaning of 'Early Childhood Services' [s.2]

■ For the purposes of s.3 summarised below, 'early childhood services' in relation to an English local authority, means:

- Early years provision
- The social services functions of the local authority, so far as relating to young children, parents or prospective parents
- Health services relating to young children, parents or prospective parents
- The provision, under arrangements made under s.2 Employment and Training Act 1973 of assistance to parents or prospective parents
- The service provided by the local authority under s.12 (duty to provide information and assistance) so far as relating to parents or prospective parents) [s.2(1)]

■ In s.2:

- 'Parent' means a parent of a young child, and includes any individual who has parental responsibility for or has care of a young child
- 'Prospective parent' means a pregnant woman or any other person who is likely to become, or is planning to become, a parent

- 'Social services functions' in relation to a local authority, has the same meaning as in the Local Authority Social Services Act 1970 [s.2(2)]

Specific Duties of Local Authority in relation to Early Childhood Services [s.3]

■ For the purpose of its general duty under s.1(1), an English local authority has the following further duties [s.3(1)].

■ The authority must make arrangements to secure that early childhood services in its area are provided in an integrated manner which is calculated to:

- Facilitate access to those services, and
- Maximise the benefit of those services to parents, prospective parents and young children [s.3(2)]

■ The authority must take steps to:

- Identify parents or prospective parents in the authority's area who would otherwise be unlikely to take advantage of early childhood services that may be of benefit to them and their young children, and
- Encourage those parents or prospective parents to take advantage of those services [s.3(3)]

■ An English local authority must take all reasonable steps to encourage and facilitate involvement in the making and implementation of arrangements under s.3 of:

- Parents and prospective parents in its area
- Early years providers in its area, including those in the private and voluntary sectors, and
- Other persons engaged in activities which may improve the well-being of young children in its area [s.3(4)]

■ In discharging its duties under s.3 an English local authority must have regard to such information about the views of young children as is available to the local authority and appears to them to be relevant to the discharge of those duties [s.3(5)].

■ In discharging its duties under s.3, an English local authority must have regard to any guidance given from time to time by the Secretary of State [s.3(6)].

NB. In s.3 'early years provider' has the same meaning as in Part 3 and 'parent' and 'prospective parent' have the same meaning as in s.2.

Duty of Local Authority and Relevant Partners to Work Together [s.4]

■ For the purposes of s.4, each of the following is a relevant partner of an English local authority:

- A Strategic Health Authority (SHA) or Primary Care Trust (PCT) for an area, any part of which falls within the area of the local authority
- The Secretary of State, in relation to her/his functions under s.2 Employment and Training Act 1973 [s.4(1)]

- An English local authority must make arrangements to work with each of its relevant partners in its performance under ss. 1 and 3 [s.4(2)].

- Each of the relevant partners of an English local authority must work with the authority and with the other relevant partners in the making of the arrangements [s.4(3)].

- An English local authority and each of its relevant partners may, for the purposes of arrangements under s.4:

  - Provide staff, goods, services, accommodation or other resources
  - Establish and maintain a 'pooled fund' [s.4(4)]

  NB. For the purposes of s.4 (4), a 'pooled fund' is one which is made up of contributions by the authority and the relevant partner or partners concerned, and out of which payments may be made towards expenditure incurred in the discharge of functions of the authority and functions of the relevant partner or partners [s.4(5)].

- An English local authority and the SHA and PCT must, in exercising their functions under s.4, have regard to any guidance given from time to time by the Secretary of State [s.4(6)].

  NB. The Secretary of State may by order amend the definition of 'early childhood services' in s. 2(1), and in connection with any amendment of that definition, make such other amendments of s.2 or 4 as appear to her/him to be necessary or expedient[s.5]

Provision of Childcare

Duty to Secure Sufficient Childcare for Working Parents [s.6]

■ An English local authority must secure, so far as is reasonably practicable, that provision of childcare (whether or not by the local authority) is sufficient to meet the requirements of parents (those with parental responsibility or actual care of a child) in its area who require childcare in order to enable them to:

- Take up, or remain in, work, or
- Undertake education or training which could reasonably be expected to assist them to obtain work [s.6(1)]

■ In determining for the above purpose whether the provision of childcare is sufficient to meet those requirements, a local authority:

- Must have regard to the needs of parents in its area for the provision of childcare in respect of which the child care element (as per s.12 Tax Credits Act 2002) of working tax credit is payable, the provision of childcare which is suitable for disabled children and
- May have regard to any childcare which they expect to be available outside its area [s.6(2)]

■ In discharging its duty under s.6 (1), a local authority must have regard to any guidance given

from time to time by the Secretary of State and s/he
may by order, modify the matters to which a local
authority must or may have regard in determining
whether the provision of childcare is sufficient
[s.6(3);(4)].

*NB. In February 2007 the DfES launched a
consultation version of guidance covering s.6
(closing date for comments 2nd May). Draft
regulations under the linked s.13(1) duty to provide
information, advice and training to childcare
providers are summarised below.*

■ Except in relation to a 'disabled' child (as per
Disability Discrimination Act 1995), s.6 does not
apply in relation to childcare for a child on or after
the 1st September next following the date on which
s/he attains the age of 14 [s.6(5)].

Duty to Secure Prescribed Early Years Provision Free of Charge [s.7]

■ An English local authority must secure that early
years provision of a prescribed description is
available free of charge for such periods as may be
prescribed for each young child in its area who:

- Has attained such age as may be prescribed, but
- Is under compulsory school age [s.7(1)]

*NB. In discharging its duty under s.7 (1), a local
authority must have regard to any guidance given
from time to time by the Secretary of State [s.7(2)]*

Powers of Local Authority in Relation to the Provision of Childcare [s.8]

- An English local authority may:

  - Assist any person who provides or proposes to provide childcare
  - Make arrangements with any other person for the provision of childcare
  - (Subject to s.8(3)), provide childcare [s.8(1)]

- The assistance which a local authority may give includes financial assistance; and the arrangements which a local authority may make include arrangements involving the provision of financial assistance by the authority [s.8(2)]

- An English local authority may not provide childcare for a particular child or group of children **unless** the local authority is satisfied:

  - That no other person is willing to provide the childcare (in pursuance of arrangements made with the authority or otherwise), or
  - If another person is willing to do so, that in the circumstances it is appropriate for the local authority to provide the childcare [s.8(3)]

- S.8 (3) does not affect the provision of childcare by the governing body of a maintained school and does not apply in relation to the provision of childcare under s.18(1) or (5) of the Children Act 1989 (day care for children in need [s.8(4);(5)].

NB. In exercising its functions under s.8, an English local authority must have regard to any guidance given from time to time by the Secretary of State [s.8(6)].

Arrangements between Local Authority and Childcare Providers [s.9]

- S.9 applies when an English local authority make arrangements with a person (other than the governing body of a maintained school) for the provision by that person of childcare in consideration of financial assistance provided by the authority [s.9(1)].

- The local authority must exercise its functions with a view to securing that the childcare provider meets any requirements imposed on her/him [s.9(2)].

- The requirements imposed by the arrangements may, in particular, if any specified conditions are not satisfied, require the repayment of the whole or any part of any financial assistance provided by the local authority under the arrangements [s.9(3)].

Charges When Local Authority Provide Childcare [s.10]

- An English local authority may enter into an agreement under which payments are made to the authority for the provision by the authority of childcare for a child [s.10 (1)].

- S.10(1) does not apply to childcare provided:

- In pursuance of the duty imposed by s.7 or
- Under s.18(1) or (5) of the Children Act 1989 (day care for children in need) for which provision about charges are made in s.29 of that Act [s.10(2)]

Duty to Assess Childcare Provision [s.11]

■ An English local authority must prepare assessments of sufficiency of the provision of childcare (whether or not by itself) in its area ('childcare assessments') [s.11(1)].

■ The first childcare assessment must be prepared before the end of the period of 1 year beginning with the commencement of s.11 [s.11(2)] (i.e. by April 2008) and subsequent assessments must be prepared at intervals not exceeding 3 years [s.11(2);(3)].

■ The authority must keep a childcare assessment prepared by it under review until the childcare assessment is superseded by a further childcare assessment [s.11 (4)].

■ Regulations (see below) may make provision requiring a childcare assessment to:

- Deal with prescribed matters or be prepared according to prescribed criteria
- Be in the prescribed form
- Be published in the prescribed manner [s.11(5)]

- In preparing a childcare assessment and keeping it under review, an English local authority must:

    - Consult such persons, or persons of such a description, as may be prescribed, and
    - Have regard to any guidance given from time to time by the Secretary of State [s.11(6)]

    NB. Except in relation to a 'disabled' child (as per Disability Discrimination Act 1995), s.11 does not apply in relation to childcare for a child on or after the 1st September next following the date on which s/he attains the age of 14 [s.11(7)].

The [Draft] Childcare (Local Authority Assessment) (England) Regulations 2006

- The above regulations define the following age ranges:

    - 2 and under
    - 3 and 4
    - 5, 6 and 7
    - 8, 9 and 10
    - 11, 12, 13 and 14
    - (in relation to disabled children only) 15, 16 and 17 [reg.2(2)]

- For the purposes of these regulations, the types of childcare are:

    - Childminding
    - Care which is available during the school term before and after the school day only

- Care which is available throughout the day in the school term and
- Care available outside of school term [reg.2(3)]

■ For the purpose of making the assessment, the local authority must divide its area into smaller geographical units (sub-local authority areas) [reg.3].

■ The assessment must include in respect of each sub-local authority area, details of:

- Number of free nursery provision places required
- Number of free nursery provision places available

■ The assessment must also include in respect of each sub-local authority area, details for each type of childcare and each age range:

- Number of places required and available
- Number of places required in respect of which the childcare element of working tax credit may be used and number of places available for which parents would be able to use the childcare element of the working tax credit
- Times at which childcare is required and is available
- Range of session lengths offered by childcare providers
- Requirements for specialist care for disabled children and those with special educational needs and the number of places available which are suitable for children who have special educational needs or require specialist care due to a disability

- • Number of vacant and unused places and
- • Range of charges for the childcare [reg.4(1)]

■ The assessment must include a summary of childcare needs which are not met in the local authority area including those that relate to:

- • Types of care available
- • Age of children for whom care is available
- • Time at which childcare is available
- • Specific needs of disabled children and
- • Location of childcare [reg.4(2)]

■ In preparing the assessment, the local authority is obliged to consult as many of the following parties as it considers appropriate:

- • Children, parents, childcare providers, and those representing them
- • Persons with an interest in childcare and those representing them
- • Persons representing local employers and employer organisations
- • Local employers
- • Neighbouring local authorities
- • Schools and further education colleges [reg.5]

■ In preparing the assessment, the local authority must consult the:

- • Local Safeguarding Children Board (LSCB)
- • Local authority's partners [reg.6]

■ Prior to publishing its summary of the assessment as required by reg.9, the local authority must make a draft available so as to allow those identified in regs. 5 and 6 an opportunity to comment on it [reg.7] and must then amend that draft in such a way as it considers appropriate [reg.8]

■ The local authority must publish a summary of the assessment on the local authority website [reg.9] and deposit such copies as it considers appropriate in public libraries, childcare settings, schools and other public places [reg.10].

■ The above summary must include the information specified in:

- Reg.4(1) in respect of the overall local authority area (detail of provision) and
- Reg.4(2) (unmet needs)

NB. Guidance and a toolkit to be applied in completing the required childcare sufficiency assessment is available from www.ecm.gov.uk

Information, Advice & Assistance

Duty to Provide Information, Advice & Assistance [s.12]

- An English local authority must establish and maintain a service providing information, advice and assistance in accordance with s.12 [s.12 (1)].

- The service must provide to parents or prospective parents information which is of a prescribed description and relates to any of the following:

  - Provision of childcare in the area of the local authority
  - Any other services or facilities, or any publications, which may be of benefit to parents or prospective parents in its area
  - Any other services or facilities, or any publications, which may be of benefit to children or young persons in its area [s.12(2)]

- In prescribing information for the purpose of s.12(2), the Secretary of State must have regard to the needs of the parents of disabled children or young persons for information relating to:

  - The provision of childcare which is suitable for disabled children, and
  - Other services or facilities, or publications, which may be of particular benefit to the parents of disabled children or young persons or to disabled children or young persons [s.12(3)]

■ The service may, in addition to providing information which it is required to provide under s.12(2), provide information relating to any of the matters mentioned in s.12(2) to such persons as the local authority considers appropriate [s.12(4)].

■ The service must provide advice and assistance to parents or prospective parents who use, or propose to use, childcare provided in the area of the local authority [s.12 (5)].

■ The service must be established and maintained in the manner which is best calculated to facilitate access to the service by persons in the local authority's area who may benefit from it, including, in particular, persons who might otherwise have difficulty in taking advantage of the service [s.12(6)].

NB. In exercising its functions under s.12, a local authority must have regard to any guidance given from time to time by the Secretary of State [s.12(7)].

■ For the purposes of s.12, a child or young person is disabled if s/he has a disability for the purposes of the Disability Discrimination Act 1995 and :

  • 'Parent' means a parent of a child or young person and includes any individual who has parental responsibility for a child, or has care of her/him
  • 'Prospective parent' means a pregnant woman or any other person who is likely to become, or is planning to become, a parent
  • 'Young person' means a person of 18 or 19 years of age [s.12(8);(9)]

The [draft] Childcare (Provision of Information) Regulations 2006

■ When a local authority provides parents/prospective parents information on the provision of childcare **in its area** in accordance with s.12(2)(a) (provision of childcare in the local authority area) that information must include the following for each provision:

- (Subject to reg. 5(2) below), contact details including the name of the provision, address, telephone number and email address
- Type of provision (group, home or school based provision)
- Age range covered
- Opening hours, the total number of weeks for which the provision is open and the specific weeks in which the provision is closed
- Number of places available for each age group
- Cost of the provision
- (In respect of early years provision), the number of places and hours covered by the free entitlement
- Whether the provision is registered on one of the registers held by the inspectorate as per s.32
- Whether the provision is inspected by the Inspectorate in accordance with Part 1 of the Education Act 2005, and if so, how parents can obtain copies of the relevant report [reg.5(1)]

■ A local authority must not provide all or any contact details of a child minder of s/he has given notice to the local authority that s/he objects [reg.5(2)]

- If the provision is based in a school, the local authority must identify whether :

    - It is run and managed by the school
    - It is run by an external contractor and registered with Her Majesty's Inspectorate for provision up to the end of the Early Years Foundation Stage; or,
    - Whether it is registered pursuant to s.63 [reg.6]

- If the provision is provided by a school other than on the school's premises, the local authority must provide information on who manages the supervised transfer arrangements [reg.7].

- If the parent is a parent of a disabled child, local authorities must provide information on access to services and specialist facilities available for disabled children within childcare settings [reg.8].

- When a local authority provides information pursuant to s.12(2)(b) (any other services/facilities/publications which may be of interest to parent/prospective parents or s.12(2)(c) (any other services/facilities/publications which may be of benefit to children/young persons in its area), the following are included as subject headings

    - Local authority/children's trust strategy
    - Education and family learning services
    - Health and wellbeing services
    - Sports/play and recreational facilities
    - Social care and family support services
    - Youth services

- Financial and Legal Services
- Child development
- Staying safe
- Local and national services for disabled children/young people

■ Where a local authority is required to provide information on any other services or facilities or any publications in accordance with s.12(2)(b) or s.12(2)(c) that information must include information in the subject headings signposted in reg.12 and detailed in the Schedule to those regulations.

■ When information is provided by the local authority on services, facilities or publications available **locally**, the information provided should, when appropriate, include the following :

- Name of the service, facility or publication
- Scope of the service, facility or publication
- Contact details of the service or facility including name of the service or facility and, where available, address, telephone number, e-mail address and web-site address
- Means of accessing the publication
- Location of the service or facility
- Type of service and facility provided
- Opening hours of the service or facility
- Cost of the service, facility or publication
- Any criteria for or restrictions on availability of the service, facility or publication [reg.13]

■ When information is provided by the local authority on services, facilities or publications **not available locally**, it is sufficient for the local authority to provide details of appropriate agencies or sources of information [reg.14]

Duty to Provide Information, Advice & Training to Childcare Providers [s.13]

■ An English local authority must, in accordance with regulations (see below), secure the provision of information, advice and training to persons:

- Providing childcare in its area who are registered under Part 3
- Who intend to provide childcare in its area in respect of which it they be required to be registered under Part 3
- Who provide childcare at any of the following schools in its area (whether or not required to be registered under Part 3) (i) a maintained school, (ii) a school approved by the Secretary of State under s.342 Education Act 1996 (approval of non-maintained special schools) and (iii) an independent school
- Who intend to provide childcare at any such school (whether or not they would be required to be registered under Part 3)
- Who are employed to assist any such persons as are mentioned in the first 3 bulleted paragraphs above in the provision of childcare or persons who intend to obtain such employment [s.13(1)]

- An English local authority may, in addition to securing the provision of information, advice and training which it is required to secure under s.13(1), provide other information, advice and training to any persons mentioned in the first 3 bulleted paragraphs above [s.13(2)]

- An English local authority **may** provide information, advice and training to persons who do not fall within the above 3 bulleted paragraphs but who:

  - Provide or intend to provide childcare in their area, or
  - Are employed to assist in the provision of childcare in its area or who intend to obtain such employment [s.13(3)]

- An English local authority may impose such charges as it considers reasonable for the provision of information, advice or training provided by it in pursuance of s.12(1) to (3) [s.13(4)].

  NB. In exercising its functions under s.13, an English local authority must have regard to any guidance given from time to time by the Secretary of State [s.13(5)].

The [draft] Childcare (Provision of Information, Advice and Training) (England) Regulations 2007

- An English local authority must secure the provision of information, advice and training for childcare providers and persons who intend to provide childcare who are/will be required to be registered under Part 3 of the Act [reg.3(1)].

■ Provision of information, advice and training must
  include:

  • Registration procedures and prescribed
    requirements for registration
  • Information on the significance of voluntary
    registration
  • Business planning, financial management and
    marketing
  • Assistance in meeting the requirements of the
    Early Years Foundation Stage (EYFS)
  • Assistance in meeting the requirements under
    any regulations made in accordance with s.59
    and s.67 of the Act
  • Assistance in meeting the requirements of the
    discrimination legislation
  • Meeting the needs of disabled children and
    other groups in accordance with reg.5
  • Effective safeguarding and promotion of
    children's welfare and compliance with statutory
    requirements, guidance and procedures for child
    protection and
  • Use of the Common Assessment Framework
    [reg.3(2)]

■ In relation to any person employed to assist in the
  provision of childcare or who intends to obtain such
  employment an English local authority must secure
  the provision of information, advice and training in
  the matters set out in regulation 3, paragraph (2)(d)-
  (i) [reg.4].

■ In relation to regulation 3, paragraph (2)(g), in
  accessing childcare in accordance with s.6 (sufficient
  childcare for working parents) information, advice
  and training must take into account the needs of:

  • Disabled children and those with special
    educational needs
  • Looked after children
  • Those using, or intending to use, childcare in
    respect of which the childcare element of the
    working tax credit is available and
  • Such children as are at risk of social exclusion
    [reg.5]

■ An English local authority must secure the provision
  of information, advice and training to a childcare
  provider:

  • (Following a report of the Chief Inspector in
    which childcare provision by such provider is
    assessed as inadequate) or
  • In respect of whom an exemption has been
    granted for a specified period of time pursuant
    to regulations made under s.46(1) of the Act;
    and such exemption is for the purposes of
    developing childcare provision to meet the
    learning and development requirements of the
    Early Years Foundation Stage [reg.6(1)]

■ An English local authority is not required to secure
  information, advice and training under the para.
  immediately above following the expiry of an
  exemption described therein [reg.6(2)].

Miscellaneous

Inspection & Powers of Secretary of State to Secure Proper Performance [ss.14; 15]

■ Ss.14 and 15 ensure that a local authority's functions under Part 1 (to improve outcomes, secure sufficient childcare and provide information) are subject to inspection by Her Majesty's Chief Inspector of Schools and subject to the powers of the Secretary of State to secure proper performance through the Education Act 1996.

Amendments to Children Act 2004 [s.16]

■ S.16 amends s.18 of the 2004 Act and provides for the appointment by English local authorities of a director of children's services (DCS) for the purpose of functions specified in that section.

■ The amendment adds functions under Part 1 of the Act to the list of those specified and thereby brings them within the responsibility of the DCS. The amendment also brings functions under Part 1 of the Act within the remit of the 'lead member' for children's services designated by the local authority under s.19 of the 2004 Act.

■ The second amendment means that functions of English local authorities under Part 1 of the Act are children's services for the purposes of ss.20 to 22 of the 2004 Act, which means that they may be subject to a joint area review (JAR) under s.20 of the 2004 Act.

NB. CAE has published a Personal Guide to the
Children Act 2004 (see appendix 3 for details)

Charges for Early Years Provision at Maintained School [s.17]

- S.17 amends s.451 of the Education Act 1996 which prohibits charges for the provision of education for registered pupils at maintained schools. The changes allow for regulations to prescribe circumstances where the prohibition on charging for education does not apply in respect of early years provision.

- The regulations may not lift the prohibition in respect of children of compulsory school age or in respect of provision that is secured under s.7 (which deals with the duty to secure free early years provision).

Part 2: General Functions of Local Authority – Wales

Provision of Childcare

Duty to Secure Sufficient Childcare for Working Parents [s.22]

■ A Welsh local authority must secure, so far as is reasonably practicable, that the provision of childcare (whether or not by that local authority) is sufficient to meet the requirements of parents (those with parental responsibility or actual care of a child) in its area who require childcare in order to enable them to:

- Take up, or remain in, work, or
- Undertake education or training which could reasonably be expected to assist them to obtain work [s.22(1)]

■ In determining for the above purpose whether the provision of childcare is sufficient to meet those requirements, a local authority:

- Must have regard to the needs of parents in its area for the provision of childcare in respect of which the child care element (as per s.12 Tax Credits Act 2002) of working tax credit is payable, the provision of childcare which is suitable for disabled children, the provision of childcare involving the use of the Welsh language and
- May have regard to any childcare which they expect to be available outside its area [s.22(2)]

*NB. In discharging its duty under s.22(1), a local
authority must have regard to any guidance given
from time to time by the Assembly which may by
order, modify the matters to which a local authority
must or may have regard in determining whether the
provision of childcare is sufficient [s.22(3);(4)].*

■ Except in relation to a 'disabled' child (as per
Disability Discrimination Act 1995), s.22 does not
apply in relation to childcare for a child on or after
the 1st September next following the date on which
s/he attains the age of 14 [s.22(5)].

Duty to Secure Sufficient Childcare for Working Parents [s.23]

■ A Welsh local authority may:

- Assist any person who provides or proposes to
  provide childcare
- Make arrangements with any other person for
  the provision of childcare
- Provide childcare

■ The assistance which a local authority may give
includes financial assistance, and the arrangements
which a local authority may make, include
arrangements involving the provision of financial
assistance by the authority [s.23 (2)].

*NB. In exercising its functions under s.23, a Welsh
local authority must have regard to any guidance
given from time to time by the Assembly [s.23(3)].*

Arrangements between Local Authority and Childcare Providers [s.24]

- S.24 applies when a Welsh local authority make arrangements with a person (other than the governing body of a maintained school) for the provision by that person of childcare in consideration of financial assistance provided by the authority [s.24(1)].

- The local authority must exercise its functions with a view to securing that the provider of the childcare meets any requirements imposed on him by the arrangements [s.24(2)].

- The requirements imposed by the arrangements may, in particular, if any specified conditions are not satisfied, require the repayment of the whole or any part of any financial assistance provided by the local authority under the arrangements [s.24(3)].

Charges when Local Authority Provide Childcare [s.25]

- A Welsh local authority may enter into an agreement under which payments are made to the authority for the provision by the authority of childcare for a child [s.25 (1)].

  NB. S.25 (1) does not apply to childcare provided under s. 18 Children Act 1989 (day care for pre-school and other children) where charging provision is made in s.29 of that Act.

Power to Require Local Authority to Assess Childcare Provision [s.26]

- The Assembly may by regulations, require a Welsh local authority to:

  - Prepare assessments at prescribed intervals of the sufficiency of the provision of childcare (whether or not by that local authority) in its area
  - Review any such assessment prepared by it [s.26(1)]

- The above regulations may make provision for the manner in which an assessment or review is to be prepared and, in particular, may require the local authority to:

  - Consult such persons, or persons of such a description, as may be prescribed, and
  - Have regard to any guidance given from time to time by the Assembly [s.26(2)]

Information, Advice & Assistance

Duty to Provide Information, Advice & Assistance [s.27]

■ A Welsh local authority must establish and maintain a service providing information, advice and assistance in accordance with s.27 and the service must provide to parents or prospective parents information which is of a prescribed description and relates to any of the following:

- The provision of childcare in the area of the local authority
- Any other services or facilities, or any publications, which may be of benefit to parents or prospective parents in its area
- Any other services or facilities, or any publications, which may be of benefit to children or young persons in its area [s.27(1);(2)]

■ In prescribing information for the purpose of s.27(2), the Assembly must have regard to the needs of the parents of disabled children/young persons for information relating to:

- The provision of childcare which is suitable for disabled children and
- Other services or facilities, or publications, which may be of particular benefit to the parents of disabled children/young persons or to disabled children/young persons [s.27(3)]

■ The service may, in addition to providing the information required by s.27(2), provide information relating to any of the matters mentioned in s.27(1) to such persons as the local authority considers appropriate [s.27(4)].

■ The service must provide advice and assistance to parents or prospective parents who use, or propose to use, childcare provided in the area of the local authority [s.27 (5)].

■ The service must be established and maintained in the manner best calculated to facilitate access to the service by those in the local authority's area who may benefit from it, including, in particular, persons who might otherwise have difficulty in taking advantage of the service [s.27(6)].

NB. In exercising its functions under s.27, a local authority must have regard to any guidance given from time to time by the Assembly [s.27(7)].

■ In s.27:

  • 'Disabled' means disabled for the purposes of the Disability Discrimination Act 1995
  • 'Parent' means a parent of a young child, and includes any individual who has parental responsibility for or has care of a young child
  • 'Prospective parent' means a pregnant woman or any other person who is likely to become, or is planning to become, a parent
  • 'Young person' means a person who is 18 or 19 years old [s.27(8);(9)]

Miscellaneous

**Inspection & Powers of Assembly to Secure
Proper Performance [s.28; 29]**

■ Ss.28 and 29 ensure that a Welsh local authority's
functions under Part 2 (to ensure sufficient childcare
and to provide information) are inspected by Her
Majesty's Chief Inspector of Education and Training
in Wales and are subject to the powers of the
Assembly to secure proper performance via
ss.496,497,497A and 497B Education Act 1996.

Part 3: Regulation of Provision of Childcare in England

General Functions of Chief Inspector [s.31]

General Functions of the Chief Inspector [s.31]

■ The Chief Inspector has the general duty of keeping the Secretary of State informed about:

- The contribution of regulated early years provision in England to the well-being of children for whom it is provided
- The quality and standards of regulated early years provision in England
- How far regulated early years provision in England meets the needs of the range of children for whom it is provided
- The quality of leadership and management in connection with regulated early years provision in England [s.31(1)]

NB. 'Regulated early years provision' means early years provision in respect of which a person is required to be registered (unless exempt from that requirement by virtue of s.34 (2) – children aged 3 or over at certain schools).

■ When asked to do so by the Secretary of State, the Chief Inspector must give advice to the Secretary of State on such matters relating to early years provision or later years provision in England as may be specified in the Secretary of State's request [s.31(3)].

■ The Chief Inspector may at any time give advice to the Secretary of State on any matter connected with:

- Early years provision or later years provision in England generally, or
- Early years provision or later years provision in England by particular persons or on particular premises [s.31(4)]

■ The Chief Inspector is to have such other functions in connection with early years provision or later years provision in England as may be assigned to her/him by the Secretary of State [s.31(5)].

Maintenance of 2 Childcare Registers [s.32]

■ The Chief Inspector must maintain 2 registers [s.32 (1)].

■ The **early years register** is a register of all persons who are required to be (and who have) registered as an 'early years provider' [s.32 (2)].

■ The **general childcare register** is divided into 2 parts:

- **Part A** is a list of childcare providers who are required to be (and who have) registered on the general register as 'later years child minders' or 'other later years providers' i.e. covering from 1st September after a child's 5th birthday up to but not including her/his 8th birthday
- **Part B** which lists all childcare providers who have been registered voluntarily

NB. In July 2006 the DfES issued a consultation paper on the rationale, requirements and inspection arrangements of the proposed 'general' (to be known as **'Ofsted Childcare register' (OCR)**). Requirements underpinning the OCR are about people, premises and provision and will apply from September 2008.

In January 2007, the DfES issued a further consultation (closing date 23rd April 2007) seeking views on proposed categories of childcare that should not be required to be registered on the early years register (for 0–5 provision) or the compulsory element of the OCR (for childcare for 6–7 year olds only).Provision that is exempt from registration will be able (if requirements can be met) to join the voluntary element of the OCR.

Regulation of Early Years Provision

Requirements to Register

Requirements to Register: Early Years Child Minders [s.33]

- A person may not provide early years childminding in England unless s/he is registered in the early years register as an early years childminder [s.33 (1)].

- The Secretary of State may by order provide that, in circumstances specified in the order, s.33(1) does not apply in relation to early years childminding i.e. s/he may exempt specified persons from requirement to be registered e.g. babysitters or nannies.

- Circumstances specified in an order under s.33(2) may relate to one or more of the following matters (among others):

  - Person providing the early years childminding
  - Child or children for whom it is provided
  - Nature of the early years childminding
  - Premises on which it is provided
  - Times during which it is provided
  - Arrangements under which it is provided

■ If it appears to the Chief Inspector that a person has provided early years childminding in contravention of s.33(1) s/he may serve an 'enforcement notice' on the person [s.33(4)].

■ An enforcement notice may be served on a person by:

• Delivering it to her/him, or
• Sending it by post [s.33(5)]

■ An enforcement notice has effect until it is revoked by the Chief Inspector [s.33 (6)].

■ A person commits an offence if, at any time when an enforcement notice has effect in relation to her/him and without reasonable excuse, s/he provides early years childminding in contravention of s.33(1) [s.33(7)].

■ A person guilty of an offence under s.33 (7) is liable on summary conviction to a fine not exceeding level 5 on the standard scale [s.33 (8)].

Requirements to Register: Other Early Years Providers [s.34]

■ Unless s/he is registered in the early years register in respect of the premises, a person may not provide:

• Early years provision on premises in England which are not domestic premises, or
• Early years provision on domestic premises in England which would be early years childminding but for s.96(5) **unless** s/he is

registered in the early years register in respect of the premises [s.34(1)]

NB. S.96(5) makes it clear that early years provision on domestic premises for reward is not early years childminding if at any time, the number of persons providing the early years provision on those premises or assisting with its provision exceeds 3.

- S.34(1) does not apply in relation to early years provision for a child/en who has (or have) attained the age of 3 if the:

  - Provision is made at any of the following schools as part of the school's activities – a maintained school, a school approved by the Secretary of State under s.342 Education Act 1996 (approval of non-maintained special schools), or an independent school,
  - Provision is made by the proprietor of the school or a person employed to work at the school, and
  - Child is a registered pupil at the school or, if the provision is made for more than one child, at least one of the children is a registered pupil at the school [s.34(2)]

- The Secretary of State may by order provide that, in circumstances specified in the order, s.34(1) does not apply in relation to early years provision [s.34(3)].

- The circumstances specified in such an order under may relate to one or more of the following matters (among others):

- • Person providing the early years provision
- • Child or children for whom it is provided
- • Nature of the early years provision
- • Premises on which it is provided

■ Times during which it is provided

■ Arrangements under which it is provided [s.34(4)]

■ A person commits an offence if, without reasonable excuse, s/he provides early years provision in contravention of s.34 (1) [s.34(5)] and if guilty of such an is liable on summary conviction to a fine not exceeding level 5 on the standard scale [s.34(6)].

Process of Registration

Applications for Registration: Early Years Childminders [s.35]

- A person who proposes to provide early years childminding in respect of which s/he is required by s. 33(1) to be registered may make an application to the Chief Inspector for registration as an early years childminder [s.35(1)].

- An application under s.35(1) must:
  - Give any prescribed information about prescribed matters
  - Give any other information which the Chief Inspector reasonably requires the applicant to give, and
  - Be accompanied by any prescribed fee [s.35(2)]

- The Chief Inspector **must grant** an application under s.35 (1) if:
  - The applicant is not disqualified from registration by regulations under s.75, and
  - It appears to the Chief Inspector that any requirements prescribed for the purposes of this subsection i.e. the 'prescribed requirements for registration' are satisfied and are likely to continue to be satisfied [s.35(3)]

- The Chief Inspector **must refuse** any application which s.35 (3) does not require her/him to grant [s.35 (4)].

- The prescribed requirements for registration may include requirements relating to:

  - Applicant
  - Premises on which the early years childminding is to be provided
  - Arrangements for early years childminding on those premises
  - Any person who may be caring for children on those premises
  - Any other person who may be on those premises [s.35(5)]

Applications for Registration: Other Early Years Providers [s.36]

- A person who proposes to provide on any premises early years provision in respect of which s/he is required by s.34(1) to be registered may make an application to the Chief Inspector for registration as an early years provider in respect of the premises.

- An application under s.36(1) must:

  - Give any prescribed information about prescribed matters
  - Give any other information which the Chief Inspector reasonably requires the applicant to give, and
  - Be accompanied by any prescribed fee [s.36(2)]

- The Chief Inspector **must grant** an application under s.36(1) if:

- The applicant is not disqualified from registration by regulations under s.75
- It appears to the Chief Inspector that any requirements prescribed for the purposes of this s.36(3) ('the prescribed requirements for registration') are satisfied and are likely to continue to be satisfied [s.36(3)]

■ The Chief Inspector **must refuse** any application which s.36 (3) does not require him to grant.

■ The 'prescribed requirements for registration' may include requirements relating to:

- The applicant;
- The premises on which the early years provision is to be provided
- The arrangements for early years provision on those premises
- Any person who may be caring for children on those premises
- Any other person who may be on those premises [s.36(5)]

Entry on the Register & Certificates [s.37]

■ If an application under s.35(1) (early years childminder) is granted, the Chief Inspector must:

- Register the applicant in the early years register as an early years childminder and
- Give the applicant a certificate of registration stating that s/he is registered [s.37(1)]

- If an application under s.36(1) (other early years provider) is granted, the Chief Inspector must:

  - Register the applicant in the early years register as an early years provider other than a childminder, in respect of the premises in question, and
  - Give the applicant a certificate of registration stating that s/he is so registered [s.37(2)]

- A certificate of registration given to the applicant must contain prescribed information about prescribed matters [s.37 (3)].

- If there is a change of circumstances which requires the amendment of a certificate of registration, the Chief Inspector must give the registered early years provider an amended certificate [s.37(4)].

- If the Chief Inspector is satisfied that a certificate of registration has been lost or destroyed, s/he must give the registered early years provider a copy, on payment by the provider of any prescribed fee [s.37(5)].

Conditions on Registration [s.38]

- The Chief Inspector may impose such conditions as s/he thinks fit on the registration of an early years provider and may do so at the time when s/he registers the person or at any subsequent time [s.38 (1) ;(2)].

■ The Chief Inspector may at any time vary or remove any condition imposed on registration [s.38 (3)].

NB. The power conferred by s.38 (1) includes power to impose conditions for the purpose of giving effect to an order under s.39 about 'learning and development requirements' or regulations under that section about 'welfare requirements' [s.38(4)].

■ A registered early years provider commits an offence if, without reasonable excuse, s/he fails to comply with any condition imposed under s.38 (1) [s.38 (5)].

■ A person guilty of an offence under s.38 (5) is liable on summary conviction to a fine not exceeding level 5 on the standard scale [s.38 (6)].

Requirements to be Met by Early Years Providers

The Early Years Foundation Stage [s.39]

- For the purpose of promoting the well-being of young children for whom early years provision is provided by those with a duty under s.40 to provide the 'Early Years Foundation Stage' (EYFS), the Secretary of State must:

  - By order specify in accordance with s.41 such requirements as s/he considers appropriate relating to learning by, and the development of, such children ('learning and development requirements'), and
  - By regulations specify in accordance with s.43 such requirements as s/he considers appropriate governing the activities of early years providers to whom s.40 applies ('welfare requirements') [s.39(1)]

- The learning and development requirements and the welfare requirements are together to be known as 'the Early Years Foundation Stage' [s.39(2)]

Duty to Implement Early Years Foundation Stage [s.40]

- S.40 applies to:

  - Early years providers providing early years provision in respect of which they are registered, and

- Early years providers providing early years provision in respect of which, but for s.34(2) (exemption for provision for children aged 3 or over at certain schools), they would be required to be registered [s.40(1)]

■ An early years provider to whom s.40 applies must:

- Secure that the early years provision meets the learning and development requirements, and
- Comply with the welfare requirements [s.40(2)]

The Learning & Development Requirements [s.41]

■ The learning and development requirements must cover the areas of learning and development specified in s.40 (3) and may specify in relation to each of the areas of learning and development the:

- Knowledge, skills and understanding which young children of different abilities and maturities are expected to have before the 1st September after their 5th birthday ('early learning goals')
- Matters, skills and processes which are required to be taught to young children of different abilities and maturities ('educational programmes'), and
- Arrangements required for assessing children for the purpose of ascertaining what they have achieved in relation to the early learning goals ('assessment arrangements') [s.41 (1);(2)].

■ The areas of learning and development are as follows –

  • Personal, social and emotional development
  • Communication, language and literacy
  • Problem solving, reasoning and numeracy
  • Knowledge and understanding of the world
  • Physical development and
  • Creative development [s.41(3)]

■ The Secretary of State may by order amend s.41(3) [s.41(4)].

■ A 'learning and development order' made under s.39(1) **may not** require the:

  • Allocation of any particular period/s of time to the teaching of any educational programme or any matter, skill or process forming part of it, or
  • Making in the timetables of any early years provider of provision of any particular kind for the periods to be allocated to such teaching [s.41(5) (6)]

Further Provisions about Assessment Arrangements [s.42]

■ A 'learning and development order' specifying assessment arrangements may confer or impose on any of the following, such functions as appear to the Secretary of State to be required:

  • An early years provider
  • The governing body or head teacher of a

maintained school in England, and

- An English local authority [s.42 (1);(2)]

■ A 'learning and development order' may specify such assessment arrangements as may for the time being, be made by a person specified in the order [s.42(3)].

■ Provision must be made for determining the extent to which any assessment arrangements, and their implementation achieve the intended purpose. Any such provision may be made by or under the learning and development order specifying the arrangements or (where the order specifies the person making the arrangements) in the arrangements themselves [s.42(4)].

■ The duties that may be imposed by virtue of s.42(1) include, in relation to persons exercising any power arising from s.42(4), the duty to permit them to:

- Enter premises on which the early years provision is provided
- Observe implementation of the arrangements, and
- Inspect, and take copies of, documents and other articles [s.42(5)]

NB. S.42(6) allows a learning and development order to provide that details of assessment arrangements may be published in a separate document and the provision made by that separate document has effect as if it had been made in the learning and development order.

Welfare Requirements [s.43]

■ The matters that may be dealt with by 'welfare regulations' made under s.39(1) include:

- The welfare of the children concerned
- The arrangements for safeguarding the children concerned
- Suitability of persons to care for, or be in regular contact with, the children concerned
- Qualifications and training
- Suitability of premises and equipment
- The manner in which the early years provision is organised
- Procedures for dealing with complaints
- The keeping of records
- The provision of information

NB. Before making welfare regulations, the Secretary of State must consult the Chief Inspector and any other persons s/he considers appropriate [s.43(2)].

■ Welfare regulations may provide that:

- A person who without reasonable excuse fails to comply with any requirement of the regulations is guilty of an offence, and
- A person guilty of the offence is liable on summary conviction to a fine not exceeding level 5 on the standard scale [s.43(3)]

Instruments Specifying Learning or Welfare Requirements [s.44]

■ A 'relevant instrument' (i.e. a learning and development order or regulations prescribing welfare requirements made under s.39(1)) may, instead of containing the provisions to be made, refer to provisions in a document published as specified in the instrument and direct that those provisions are to have effect/have effect as specified in the instrument [s.44(1)].

■ A 'relevant instrument' may also confer powers and impose duties on the Chief Inspector in the exercise of her/his functions under Part 3 of this Act and in particular may require her/him to have regard to factors, standards and other matters prescribed by or referred to in the instrument [s.44(2);(3)]

■ If a relevant instrument requires any person (other than the Chief Inspector) to have regard to or meet factors, standards and other matters prescribed by or referred to in the instrument, the instrument may also provide for any allegation that the person has failed to do so to be taken into account:

- By the Chief Inspector in the exercise of his functions under this Part, or
- In any proceedings under Part 3 of this Act [s.44(4)]

Procedure for Making Certain Orders [s.45]

■ If the Secretary of State proposes to make a learning and development order under s.39(1) specifying early learning goals or educational programmes, s/he must give notice of the proposal, and give a reasonable opportunity of submitting evidence and representations as to the issues arising, to:

- Such bodies representing the interests of early years providers as the Secretary of State considers appropriate, and
- Any other persons with whom consultation appears to the Secretary of State to be desirable [s.45(1);(2)]

■ When the Secretary of State has considered any evidence and representations submitted, s/he he must publish in such manner as s/he thinks is likely to bring them to the notice of persons having a special interest in early years provision, a:

- Draft of the proposed order and any associated document, and
- Summary of the views expressed during the consultation [s.45(3)]

■ The Secretary of State must allow a period of not less than one month beginning with the publication of the draft of the proposed order for the submission of any further evidence and representations and when that period has expired, s/he may make the order, with or without modifications [s.45(4);(5)].

Power to Enable Exemptions to be Conferred [s.46]

■ Regulations may enable the Secretary of State, in prescribed circumstances, to direct in respect of a particular early years provider or a particular description of early years providers, that to such extent as may be prescribed the learning and development requirements:

- • Do not apply, or
- • Apply with such modifications as may be specified in the direction [s.46(1)]

■ Regulations may enable an early years provider, in prescribed circumstances, to determine in respect of a particular young child that to such extent as may be prescribed the learning and development requirements:

- • Do not apply, or
- • Apply with such modifications as may be specified in the determination [s.46(2)]

NB. S.47(1) amends s.157 Education Act 2002 so that the independent school standards prescribed by regulations made under that section do not apply in relation to early years provision for pupils of independent schools aged less than 3. Independent schools providing early years provision for children under 3 are required to be registered under Part 3 of the Childcare Act 2006 and to implement the Early Years Foundation Stage.

Inspection

Inspections [s.49]

- For registered early years providers, the Chief Inspector:

  - Must at such intervals as may be prescribed inspect early years provision to which this section applies,
  - Must inspect early years provision to which this section applies at any time when the Secretary of State requires the Chief Inspector to secure its inspection, and
  - May inspect early years provision to which this section applies at any other time when the Chief Inspector considers that it would be appropriate for it to be inspected [s.49(1);(2)]

- Regulations may provide that in prescribed circumstances the Chief Inspector is **not** required to inspect early years provision at an interval prescribed in s.49(2)] e.g. the provision has no children

- Regulations may provide that the Chief Inspector is not required by s.49(2) to inspect early years provision at an independent school if the early years provision is inspected in prescribed circumstances by a body approved by the Secretary of State for the purposes of this section [s.49(4)].

- A requirement made by the Secretary of State for the Chief Inspector to inspect as per s.49(2) may be imposed in relation to particular premises or a class of premises [s.49(5)].

■ Regulations may make provision requiring the registered person to notify prescribed persons of the fact that early years provision is to be inspected under s.49 [s.49(6)]

NB. If the Chief Inspector so elects, s/he may determine that an inspection completed at the request of the Secretary of State or at her/his own discretion may be counted as though it were one satisfying the obligation to inspect at prescribed intervals [s.49(7)].

Report of Inspection [s.50]

■ After conducting an inspection under s.49, the Chief Inspector must make a report in writing on the:

- Contribution of the early years provision to the well-being of the children for whom it is provided
- Quality and standards of the early years provision,
- How far the early years provision meets the needs of the range of children for whom it is provided, and
- Quality of leadership and management in connection with the early years provision [s.50(1)]

- The Chief Inspector:

  - May send a copy of the report to the Secretary of State and must do so without delay if the Secretary of State requests a copy
  - Must ensure that a copy of the report is sent without delay to the registered person
  - Must ensure that copies of the report, or such parts of it as s/he considers appropriate, are sent to such other persons as may be prescribed, and
  - May arrange for the report (or parts of it) to be further published in any manner s/he considers appropriate [s.50(2)]

- Regulations may make provision:

  - Requiring the registered person to make a copy of any report sent to her/him under s.50(2) available for inspection by prescribed persons
  - Requiring the registered person, except in prescribed cases, to provide a copy of the report to prescribed persons
  - Authorising the registered person in prescribed cases to charge a fee for providing a copy of the report [s.50(3)]

NB. S.50(4) has the effect of allowing the Chief Inspector to publish the report by electronic means and provides for reports to be 'privileged' for the purposes of defamation unless they have been made with malice.

Regulation of Later Years Provision for Children under 8

Requirements to Register

Requirement to Register: Later Years Childminders for Children under 8 [s.52]

- A person may not provide 'later years childminding' in England for a child under the age of eight unless s/he is registered in Part A of the general childcare register as a childminder [s.52(1)].

- The Secretary of State may by order provide that, in circumstances specified in the order, s.52(1)) does not apply in relation to later years childminding.

- The circumstances specified in an order under s.52(2) may relate to one or more of the following matters (among others):

  - Person providing the later years childminding
  - Child or children for whom it is provided
  - Nature of the later years childminding
  - Premises on which it is provided
  - Times during which it is provided
  - Arrangements under which it is provided [s.52(3)]

- If it appears to the Chief Inspector that a person has provided later years childminding in contravention of s.52(1), s/he may serve a notice ('an enforcement notice') on the person [s.52(4)].

- An enforcement notice may be served on a person by:

  - Delivering it to her/him, or
  - Sending it by post [s.52(5)]

- An enforcement notice has effect until it is revoked by the Chief Inspector [s.52 (6)].

- A person commits an offence if, at any time when an enforcement notice has effect in relation to her/him and without reasonable excuse, s/he provides later years childminding in contravention of s.52(1) [s.52(7)].

- A person guilty of an offence under s.52(7) is liable on summary conviction to a fine not exceeding level 5 on the standard scale [s.52(8)].

Requirement to Register: Other Later Years Providers for Children Under 8 [s.53]

- A person **may not** (unless registered in Part A of the general childcare register in respect of the premises) provide for a child under the age of eight:

  - Later years provision on premises in England which are not domestic premises, or
  - Later years provision on domestic premises in England which would be later years childminding but for s.96(9) (which imposes a maximum of 3 providers or assistants if the service is to be regarded as later years childminding) [s.53(1)]

- S.53(1) does not apply in relation to later years provision for a child if the:

  - Provision is made as part of the school's activities at a maintained school, a school approved by the Secretary of State under s. 342 Education Act 1996 (approval of non-maintained special schools), or an independent school or
  - Provision is made by the school's proprietor or a person employed to work at the school, **and** the
  - Child is a registered pupil at the school or, if the provision is made for more than one child under 8, at least one of the children is a registered pupil at the school [s.53(2)]

- The Secretary of State may by order provide, in circumstances specified in the order, that s.53(1) does not apply in relation to later years provision and those may relate to one or more of the following matters (among others):

  - Person providing the later years provision
  - Child or children for whom it is provided
  - Nature of the later years provision
  - Premises on which it is provided
  - Times during which it is provided
  - Arrangements under which it is provided [s.53(3);(4)]

■   A person commits an offence if, without reasonable excuse, s/he provides later years provision in contravention of s.53(1) and a person guilty of an offence under s.53(5) is liable on summary conviction to a fine not exceeding level 5 on the standard scale [s.53(5);(6)].

Process of Registration

Applications for Registration: Later Years Childminders [s.54]

■ A person who proposes to provide later years childminding in respect of which s/he is required by s.52(1) to be registered may make an application to the Chief Inspector for registration as a later years childminder [s.54(1)].

■ An application under s.54(1) must:

- Give any prescribed information about prescribed matters
- Give any other information which the Chief Inspector reasonably requires the applicant to give, and
- Be accompanied by any prescribed fee [s.54(2)]

■ The Chief Inspector **must grant** an application under s.54 (1) if:

- The applicant is not disqualified from registration by regulations under s.75, and
- It appears to the Chief Inspector that the 'prescribed requirements for registration' are satisfied and are likely to continue to be satisfied [s.54(3)]

■ The Chief Inspector must refuse any application under s.54 (1) which s.54 (3) does not require her/him to grant [s.54(4)].

■ The prescribed requirements for registration may include requirements relating to:

- The applicant
- The premises on which the later years childminding is to be provided
- The arrangements for later years childminding on those premises
- Any person who may be caring for children on those premises
- Any other person who may be on those premises [s.54(5)]

Applications for Registration: Other Later Years Providers [s.55]

■ A person who proposes to provide on any premises, later years provision in respect of which s/he is required by s.53(1) to be registered, may make an application to the Chief Inspector for registration as a later years provider in respect of the premises.

■ An application under s.55(1) must:

- Give any prescribed information about prescribed matters
- Give any other information which the Chief Inspector reasonably requires the applicant to give, and
- Be accompanied by any prescribed fee [s.55(2)]

■ The Chief Inspector **must grant** an application under s.55(1) if:

- • The applicant is not disqualified from registration by regulations under s.75, and
- • It appears to the Chief Inspector that any requirements prescribed for the purposes of 'the prescribed requirements for registration' are satisfied and are likely to continue to be satisfied [s.55(3)]

■ The Chief Inspector must refuse any application under s.55(1) which s.55 (3) does not require her/him to grant.

■ The prescribed requirements for registration may include requirements relating to:

- • The applicant
- • The premises on which the later years provision is to be provided
- • The arrangements for later years provision on those premises
- • Any person who may be caring for children on those premises
- • Any other person who may be on those premises [s.55(5)]

Entry on the Register and Certificates [s.56]

■ If an application under s.54(1) (later years childminding) is granted, the Chief Inspector must:

- • Register the applicant in Part A of the general childcare register as a later years childminder, and
- • Give the applicant a certificate of registration stating that s/he is so registered [s.56(1)]

- Register the person in Part A of the general childcare register as a later years childminder, and
- Give the person a certificate of registration stating that s/he is so registered [s.57(1)]

■ If a person who is registered in the early years register in respect of particular premises as an early years provider other than a childminder gives notice to the Chief Inspector that s/he proposes to provide later years provision in respect of which s/he is required to be registered under on the same premises, the Chief Inspector must:

- Register the person in Part A of the general childcare register as a later years provider other than a childminder, in respect of the premises, and
- Give the person a certificate of registration stating that s/he is so registered [s.57(2)]

NB. Provisions about information to be contained in certificates, amendments and about lost or stolen certificates are the same as s.56(3)-(5) above [s.57(3)]

- If an application under s.55(1) (other later
  providers) is granted, the Chief Inspector m

  - Register the applicant in Part A of the g
    childcare register as a later years provide
    than a childminder, in respect of the pre
    question, and
  - Give the applicant a certificate of registra
    stating that s/he is so registered [s.56(2)

- In either of the above cases, a certificate of
  registration given to the applicant must contai
  prescribed information about prescribed matte
  [s.56(3)]

- If there is a change of circumstances which requ
  the amendment of a certificate of registration, t
  Chief Inspector must give the registered later yea
  provider an amended certificate [s.56(4)].

- If the Chief Inspector is satisfied that a certificate
  registration has been lost or destroyed, the Chief
  Inspector must give the registered later years
  provider a copy, on payment by the provider of an
  prescribed fee [s.56(5)].

Special Procedure for Registered Early Years Providers [s.57]

- If a person who is registered in the early years
  register as an early years childminder gives notice to
  the Chief Inspector that s/he proposes to provide
  later years childminding in respect of which s/he is
  required to be registered, the Chief Inspector must:

Regulation

Conditions on Registration [s.58]

- The Chief Inspector may impose such conditions as s/he thinks fit on the registration of a later years provider and this power may be exercised at the time when the Chief Inspector registers the person in pursuance of s.56 or 57 or at any subsequent time [s.58 (1); (2)].

- The Chief Inspector may at any time vary or remove any such condition [s.58(3)].

- The Chief Inspector's power includes power to impose conditions for the purpose of giving effect to regulations under s.59 (regulations governing activities) [s.58(4)].

- A registered later years provider commits an offence if, without reasonable excuse, s/he fails to comply with any condition imposed [s.58(5)] .

- A person guilty of such an offence is liable on summary conviction to a fine not exceeding level 5 on the standard scale [s.58(6)].

Regulations Governing Activities [s.59]

- S.59 applies to:

  - Later years providers providing later years provision in respect of which they are registered under and

- Later years providers providing later years provision in respect of which, but for s.53(2) (exemption for provision for children at certain schools), they would be required to be registered [s.59(1)]

■ The Secretary of State may, after consulting the Chief Inspector and any other person s/he considers appropriate, make regulations governing the activities of later years providers to whom s.59 applies.

■ The regulations may deal with the following matters (among others):

- Welfare of the children concerned
- Arrangements for safeguarding the children concerned
- Suitability of persons to care for, or be in regular contact with, the children concerned
- Qualifications and training
- Suitability of premises and equipment
- Manner in which the later years provision is organised
- Procedures for dealing with complaints
- Keeping of records
- Provision of information [s.59(3)]

■ The power to make regulations under s.59 may be exercised so as confer powers or impose duties on the Chief Inspector in the exercise of her/his functions under Part 3 of this Act, and in particular, to have regard to factors, standards and other

matters prescribed by or referred to in the
regulations [s.59(4);(5)].

■ If the regulations require any person (other than the
Chief Inspector) to have regard to or to meet factors,
standards and other matters prescribed by or
referred to in the regulations, they may also provide
for any allegation that the person has failed to do so
to be taken into account:

- By the Chief Inspector in the exercise of her/his
functions or
- In any proceedings Part 3 [s.59(6)]

■ The regulations may provide that:

- A person who without reasonable excuse fails to
comply with any requirement of the regulations
is guilty of an offence, and
- A person guilty of the offence is liable on
summary conviction to a fine not exceeding level
5 on the standard scale [s.59 (7)].

Inspection

Inspections [s.60]

■ For later years provision in respect of which the provider is registered, the Chief Inspector:

- Must inspect later years provision to which this section applies at any time when the Secretary of State requires the Chief Inspector to secure its inspection, and
- May inspect later years provision to which s.60 applies at any other time when the Chief Inspector considers that it would be appropriate for it to be inspected [s.60(1);(2)]

■ A requirement made by the Secretary of State as above may be imposed in relation to later years provision at particular premises or a class of premises [s.60(3)].

■ Regulations may make provision requiring the registered person to notify prescribed persons of the fact that later years provision is to be inspected under this section [s.60(4)]

Reports of Inspections [s.61]

■ After conducting an inspection under s.60, the Chief Inspector may make a report in writing on such of the following matters as s/he considers appropriate:

- Contribution of the later years provision to the well-being of the children for whom it is provided

- Quality and standards of the later years provision
- How far the later years provision meets the needs of the range of children for whom it is provided
- Quality of leadership and management in connection with the later years provision [s.61(1)]

■ The Chief Inspector:

- May send a copy of the report to the Secretary of State and must do so without delay if the Secretary of State requests a copy
- Must ensure that a copy of the report is sent without delay to the registered person
- Must ensure that copies of the report, or such parts of it as s/he considers appropriate, are sent to such other persons as may be prescribed, and
- May arrange for the report (or parts of it) to be further published in any manner s/he considers appropriate [s.61(2)]

■ Regulations may make provision:

- Requiring the registered person to make a copy of any inspection report sent to him under available for inspection by prescribed persons
- Requiring the registered person, except in prescribed cases, to provide a copy of the report to prescribed persons
- Authorising the registered person in prescribed cases to charge a fee for providing a copy of the report [s.61(3)]

Voluntary Registration

Process of Voluntary Registration

Applications for Registration on the General Register: Childminders [s.62]

■ A person may make an application to the Chief Inspector for registration in Part B of the general childcare register as a childminder if s/he provides or proposes to provide in England:

- Later years childminding for a child who has attained the age of eight, or
- Early years childminding or later years childminding for a child who has not attained that age but in respect of which the person is not required to be registered

■ Such an application must:

- Give any prescribed information about prescribed matters
- Give any other information which the Chief Inspector reasonably requires the applicant to give
- Be accompanied by any prescribed fee [s.62(2)]

■ The Chief Inspector **must grant** such an application if:

- The applicant is not disqualified from registration by regulations under s.75, and

- It appears to the Chief Inspector that any 'prescribed requirements for registration' are satisfied and are likely to continue to be satisfied [s.62(3)]

■ The Chief Inspector **must refuse** any such application she is not required by s.62 (3)] to grant [s.62 (4)].

■ The prescribed requirements for registration may include requirements relating to:

- Applicant
- Premises on which the childminding is being (or is to be) provided
- Arrangements for childminding on those premises
- Any person who may be caring for children on those premises
- Any other person who may be on those premises [s.62(5)]

Applications for Registration on the General Register: Other Childcare Providers [s.63]

■ A person may make an application to the Chief Inspector for registration in Part B of the general childcare register in respect of the premises if a person who provides or proposes to provide on premises in England:

- Later years provision (other than later years childminding) for a child who has attained the age of eight, or

- Early years provision or later years provision (other than early years or later years childminding) for a child who has not attained that age but in respect of which the person is not required to be registered [s.63(1)]

■ Such an application must:

- Give any prescribed information about prescribed matters
- Give any other information which the Chief Inspector reasonably requires the applicant to give
- Be accompanied by any prescribed fee [s.63(2)]

■ Such an application may not be made in respect of provision for a child aged three or over if the:

- Provision is made at any of the following as part of its activities – a maintained school, a school approved by the Secretary of State under s.342 Education Act 1996 (approval of non-maintained special schools), or an independent school,
- Provision is made by the proprietor of the school or a person employed to work at the school, and
- Child is a registered pupil at the school or, if the provision is made for more than one child who has attained the age of three, at least one of the children is a registered pupil at the school [s.63(3)]

■ The Chief Inspector **must grant** an application under s.63(1) if:

- The applicant is not disqualified from registration by regulations under s.75, **and**
- It appears to the Chief Inspector that any requirements 'prescribed requirements for registration' are satisfied and are likely to continue to be satisfied [s.63(4)]

■ The Chief Inspector **must refuse** any application under s.63(1) which s.63(4) does not require her/him to grant [s.63(5)].

■ The prescribed requirements for registration may include requirements relating to:

- Applicant
- Premises on which the childcare is being (or is to be) provided
- Arrangements for childcare on those premises
- Any person who may be caring for children on those premises
- Any other person who may be on those premises [s.63(6)]

Entry on the Register & Certificates [s.64]

■ If an application under s.62(1) (voluntary registration childminder) is granted, the Chief Inspector must:

- Register the applicant in Part B of the general childcare register as a childminder, and
- Give the applicant a certificate of registration stating that s/he is so registered [s.64 (1)]

- If an application under s.63(1) (voluntary registration other childcare provider) is granted, the Chief Inspector must:

  - Register the applicant in Part B of the general childcare register as a provider of childcare other than a childminder, in respect of the premises in question, and
  - Give the applicant a certificate of registration stating that s/he is so registered [s.64(2)]

- A certificate of registration given to the applicant in pursuance of s.64(1) or s.63(2) must contain prescribed information about prescribed matters [s.64(3)].

- If there is a change of circumstances which requires the amendment of a certificate of registration, the Chief Inspector must give the registered person an amended certificate [s.64(5)].

- If the Chief Inspector is satisfied that a certificate of registration has been lost or destroyed, the Chief Inspector must give the registered person a copy, on payment by the provider of any prescribed fee [s.64(5)].

Special Procedure for Persons Already Registered [s.65]

- If a person who is registered **as a childminder** in the early years register or in Part A of the general childcare register gives notice to the Chief Inspector that s/he wishes to be registered in Part

B of the general childcare register, the Chief Inspector must:

- Register the person in Part B of the general childcare register as a childminder, and
- Give the applicant a certificate of registration stating that s/he is so registered [s.65(1)]

■ If a person who is registered (**otherwise than as a childminder**) in the early years register or in Part A of the general childcare register in respect of particular premises gives notice to the Chief Inspector that s/he wishes to be registered in Part B of the general childcare register in respect of the same premises, the Chief Inspector must:

- Register the person in Part B of the general childcare register as a provider of childcare other than a childminder, in respect of the premises, and
- Give the person a certificate of registration stating that s/he is so registered [s.65(2)]

NB. Provisions about information to be contained in certificates, amendments and about lost or stolen certificates are the same as s.64(3)–(5) above [s.65(3)].

Regulation of Persons Registering Voluntarily

Conditions on Registration [s.66]

- The Chief Inspector may impose such conditions as s/he thinks fit on the registration of a person seeking to register voluntarily and her/his power to do so may be exercised at the time when s/he registers a person in pursuance of ss. 64 or 65 or at any subsequent time. [s.66(1);(2)].

- The Chief Inspector may at any time vary or remove any such condition [s.66 (3)].

- The power conferred bys.66 (1) includes power to impose conditions for the purpose of giving effect to regulations under s.67 (regulations governing activities) [s.66 (4)].

- A voluntarily registered person commits an offence if, without reasonable excuse, s/he fails to comply with any condition imposed under s.66 (1) [s.66 (5)].

- A person guilty of an offence under s.66 (5) is liable on summary conviction to a fine not exceeding level 5 on the standard scale [s.66 (6)].

Regulations Governing Activities [s.67]

- For persons providing early years provision or later years provision (or both) in respect of which they are voluntarily registered, the Secretary of State may, after consulting the Chief Inspector and any other person s/he considers appropriate, make regulations governing the activities of those persons [s.67(1);(2)].

- The regulations may deal with the following matters (among others):

  - Welfare of the children concerned
  - Arrangements for safeguarding the children concerned
  - Suitability of persons to care for, or be in regular contact with, the children concerned
  - Qualifications and training
  - Suitability of premises and equipment
  - Manner in which the childcare provision is organised
  - Procedures for dealing with complaints
  - Keeping of records
  - Provision of information [s.67(3)]

- The power to make regulations under s.67 may be exercised so as confer powers or impose duties on the Chief Inspector in the exercise of her/his functions under Part 3 and in particular, may be so exercised so as to require her/him to have regard to factors, standards and other matters prescribed by or referred to in the regulations [s.67 (4);(5)].

- If the regulations require any person (other than the Chief Inspector) to have regard to or meet factors, standards and other matters prescribed by or referred to in the regulations, they may also provide for any allegation that the person has failed to do so to be taken into account:

- By the Chief Inspector in the exercise of her/his functions under Part 3, or
- In any proceedings under this Part [s.67(6)]

Common Provisions

Cancellation of Registration etc

Cancellation of Registration [s.68]

- The Chief Inspector **must cancel** the registration of an early or later years provider or voluntarily registered childminder/other childcare provider **if** it appears to her/him that the person has become disqualified from registration by regulations under s.75 [s.68(1)].

- The Chief Inspector **may cancel** the registration of any such person if it appears to her/him that:

  - The prescribed requirements for registration which apply in relation to the person's registration have ceased, or will cease, to be satisfied,
  - The person has failed to comply with a condition imposed on her/his registration
  - S/he has failed to comply with a requirement imposed on her/him by regulations
  - In the case of a person registered as an early years provider, s/he has failed to comply with the learning and development requirements of s.40(2)
  - In any case, that s/he has failed to pay a prescribed fee [s.68(2)]

- The Chief Inspector **may cancel** the registration of a person registered as an early years childminder under if it appears to her/him that the person has not provided early years childminding for a period of more than three years during which s/he was registered [s.68(3)].

- The Chief Inspector **may cancel** the registration of a person registered as a later years childminder under if it appears to her/him that the person has not provided later years childminding for a period of more than three years during which s/he was registered [s.68(4)].

- The Chief Inspector may cancel the registration of a person voluntarily registered as a childminder under if it appears to her/him that s/he has provided neither early years childminding nor later years childminding for a period of more than three years during which s/he was registered [s.68(5)].

- If a requirement to make any changes or additions to any services, equipment or premises has been imposed on a registered person, registration may not be cancelled on the ground of any defect or insufficiency in the services, equipment or premises if:

  - The time set for complying with the requirements has not expired, and
  - It is shown that the defect or insufficiency is due to the changes or additions not having been made [s.68(6)]

Suspension of Registration [s.69]

- Regulations may provide for the registration of a person to be suspended for a prescribed period in prescribed circumstances and must include provision conferring on the registered person a right of appeal to the Tribunal against suspension [s.69(1);(2)].

- A person registered as an early years childminder under may not provide early years childminding in England at any time when her/his registration is suspended in accordance with regulations under this section [s.69(3)].

- A person registered as a later years childminder under may not provide later years childminding in England, for a child who has not attained the age of eight, at any time when her/his registration is suspended in accordance with regulations under this section [s.69(4)].

  NB. S..69 (3) and s.69(4) do not apply in relation to early years childminding or(as the case may be) later years childminding which the person may provide without being registered[s.69(5)].

- A person registered as an early years provider (other than an early years childminder) may not provide early years provision on premises in England at any time when her/his registration in respect of the premises is suspended in accordance with regulations under this section [s.69(6)].

- A person registered as a later years provider (other than a later years childminder) may not provide later years provision on premises in England, for a child who has not attained the age of eight, at any time when her/his registration in respect of the premises is suspended in accordance with regulations under this section [s.69(7)].

NB. S.69(6) and s.69(7) do not apply in relation to early years provision or (as the case may be) later years provision which the person may provide without being registered [s.69(8)].

- A person commits an offence if, without reasonable excuse, s/he contravenes s.69 (3), (4), (6) or (7) [s.69 (9)].

- A person guilty of an offence under s.69 (9) is liable on summary conviction to a fine not exceeding level 5 on the standard scale [s.69 (10).

Voluntary Removal from Register [s.70]

- A person registered as an early years childminder/other early years provider/later years childminder/other later years provider or voluntarily registered may give notice to the Chief Inspector that s/he wishes to be removed from the early years register or (as the case may be) from Part A or B of the general childcare register [s.70(1)].

- If a person gives such notice the Chief Inspector **must** remove her/him from the early years register or (as the case may be) from the relevant Part of the general childcare register [s.70 (2)].

- The Chief Inspector **must not** act under s.70(2) if the Chief Inspector has:

  - Sent the person a notice (in pursuance of s.73(2)) of her/his intention to cancel her/his registration, and
  - Has not decided that s/he no longer intends to take that step [s.70(3)]

- The Chief Inspector must not act under s.70(2) if:

  - The Chief Inspector has sent the person a notice (in pursuance of s.73(7)) of her/his decision to cancel her/his registration, and
  - The time within which an appeal under s.74 may be brought has not expired or, if such an appeal has been brought, it has not been determined [s.70(4)]

- S.70(3) and s.70 (4) do not apply if the person is seeking removal from Part B of the general childcare register [s.70(5)].

  NB. Regulations may make provision requiring the Chief Inspector to remove a registered person from Part B of the general childcare register on the expiry of a prescribed period of time from the date of her/his registration [s.71].

Cancellation etc in an Emergency

Protection of Children in an Emergency [s.72]

■ In relation to a registered person registered the Chief Inspector may apply to a justice of the peace (JP) for an order:

- Cancelling the person's registration
- Varying or removing a condition to which her/his registration is subject
- Imposing a new condition on her/his registration [s.72(1)]

■ If it appears to JP that a child for whom early years provision or later years provision is being or may be provided by that person 'is suffering or is likely to suffer significant harm', the JP may make the order [s.72(2)].

■ An application under s.72(1) may be made without notice [s.72(3)].

■ An order under s.72 (2):

- Must be made in writing, and
- Has effect from the time when it is made [s.72(4)]

■ If an order is made under s.72(2), the Chief Inspector must serve on the registered person as soon as is reasonably practicable after the making of the order:

- A copy of the order

- A copy of any written statement in support of
  the application for the order, and
- Notice of any right of appeal conferred by s.74
  [s.72(5)]

■ The documents mentioned in s.72(5) may be served
on the registered person by:

- Delivering them to her/him, or
- Sending them by post [s.72(6)]

*NB. For the purposes of this section, 'harm' has the
same meaning as in the Children Act 1989 and the
question of whether harm is significant is to be
determined in accordance with s.31(10) of that Act
(CAE publishes a guide to the Children Act 1989 –
see appendix 3 for details).*

Registration: Procedural Safeguards

Protection for Taking Certain Steps [s.73]

■ S.73 applies if the Chief Inspector proposes to take any of the following steps:

- Refuse an application for registration
- Impose a new condition on a person's registration
- Vary or remove any condition imposed on a person's registration
- Refuse to grant an application for the variation or removal of any such condition
- Cancel a person's registration [s.73(1)]

■ The Chief Inspector must give to the applicant or (as the case may be) the registered person notice of her/his intention to take the step in question [s.73(2)]

■ The notice must:

- Give the Chief Inspector's reasons for proposing to take the step, and
- Inform the person concerned of her/his rights under s.73 [s.73(3)]

■ The Chief Inspector may not take the step until the end of the period of 14 days beginning with the day on which s/he gives notice under s.73(2), unless the applicant or (as the case may be) the registered person notifies the Chief Inspector that s/he does not wish to object to the step being taken [s.73(4)]

■ If the 'recipient' of a notice under s.73 (2) gives notice to the Chief Inspector that s/he wishes to object to the step being taken, the Chief Inspector must give her/him an opportunity to object before deciding whether to take the step [s.73(5)].

■ An objection made in pursuance of s.73(5) may be made orally or in writing and in either case may be made by the recipient or her/his representative [s.73(6)].

■ If the Chief Inspector decides to take the step, s/he must give the recipient notice of her/his decision (whether or not the recipient informed the Chief Inspector that s/he wished to object to the step being taken) [s.73(7)].

■ The taking of a step to impose a new condition on a person's registration, vary or remove any condition imposed on a person's registration or to cancel a person's registration under s.73(1) does not have effect until:

  • Expiry of the time within which an appeal may be brought under s.74, or
  • If such an appeal is brought, the time when the appeal is determined (and the taking of the step is confirmed) [s.73(8)]

■ S.73(8) does not prevent such a step having effect before the expiry of the time within which an appeal may be brought if the person concerned notifies the Chief Inspector that s/he does not intend to appeal [s.73(9)].

■ If the Chief Inspector gives notice to an applicant for registration that s/he intends to refuse the application, the application may not be withdrawn without the consent of the Chief Inspector [s.73 (10)].

NB. In s.73 and s.74, 'a new condition' means a condition imposed otherwise than at the time of the person's registration [s.73 (11)].

Appeals [s.74]

■ An applicant for registration or (as the case may be) a registered person may appeal to the Tribunal against the taking of any of the following steps by the

■ Chief Inspector under Part 3:

- Refusal of his application for registration
- Imposition of a new condition on her/his registration
- Variation or removal of any condition imposed on her/his registration
- Refusal of an application to vary or remove any such condition
- Cancellation of her/his registration [s.74(1)]

■ An applicant for registration or (as the case may be) a registered person may also appeal to the Tribunal against any other determination made by the Chief Inspector under Part 3 which is of a prescribed description [s.74(2)].

■ A person against whom an order is made under s.72(2) may appeal to the Tribunal against the making of the order [s.74(3)].

■ On an appeal the Tribunal must either:

- Confirm the taking of the step, the making of the other determination or the making of the order (as the case may be), or
- Direct that it shall not have, or shall cease to have, effect [s.74(4)]

■ Unless the Tribunal has confirmed the taking of refusal of application for registration, cancellation of registration or the making of an order under s.72(2) cancelling a person's registration, the Tribunal may also do either or both of the following:

- Impose conditions on the registration of the person concerned
- Vary or remove any condition previously imposed on her/his registration [s.74(5)]

Disqualification from Registration

Disqualification from Registration [s.75]

■ Regulations may provide for a person to be 'disqualified' from registration and may, in particular, provide for a person to be disqualified from registration if:

- S/he is included in the list kept under s.1 Protection of Children Act 1999
- S/he is subject to a direction under s.142 Education Act 2002 on the grounds that s/he is unsuitable to work with children or on grounds relating to health
- An order of a prescribed kind has been made at any time with respect to her/him
- An order of a prescribed kind has been made at any time with respect to a child who has been in her/his care
- A requirement of a prescribed kind has been imposed at any time with respect to such a child, under or by virtue of any enactment
- S/he has at any time been refused registration under this Act or under Part 10 or Part 10A of the Children Act 1989 or any prescribed enactment, or had any such registration cancelled
- S/he has been convicted of an offence of a prescribed kind or has been discharged absolutely or conditionally for such an offence
- S/he has been given a caution in respect of an offence of a prescribed kind

- S/he has at any time been disqualified from fostering a child privately (within the meaning of the Children Act 1989)
- A prohibition has been imposed on him at any time under s.69 Children Act 1989, s.10 Foster Children (Scotland) Act 1984 or any prescribed enactment
- Her/his rights and powers with respect to a child have at any time been vested in a prescribed authority under a prescribed enactment [s.75(1)-(3)]

■ Regulations may provide for a person to be disqualified from registration if s/he lives in:

- The same household as another person who is disqualified from registration, or
- A household in which any such person is employed [s.75(4)]

■ Regulations under s.75(2) or s.75(4) may provide for a person not to be disqualified from registration (and in particular not to be disqualified from registration for the purposes of s.76 by reason of any fact which would otherwise cause her/him to be disqualified if:

- S/he has disclosed the fact to the Chief Inspector, and
- The Chief Inspector has consented in writing to the person's not being disqualified from registration and has not withdrawn her//his consent [s.75(5)]

NB. In s.75, 'caution' includes a reprimand or warning within the meaning of s.65 Crime and Disorder Act 1998 and 'enactment' means any enactment having effect at any time in any part of the UK [s.75(6)]. A conviction in respect of which a probation order was made before 01.10.92 (which would not otherwise be treated as a conviction) is to be treated as a conviction for the purposes of s.75 [s.75 (7)].

Consequences of Disqualification [s.76]

- This section applies to:

  - Early years provision in respect of which the provider is required by s.33(1) (childminder)or s.34(1) (other early years provider) to be registered
  - Early years provision in respect of which, but for s.34(2) (exemptions with respect to those aged three and over in specified schools/circumstances), the provider would be required to be registered
  - Later years provision in respect of which the provider is required by s.52(1) (childminder) or 53(1) (other later years provider) to be registered, and
  - Later years provision in respect of which, but for s.53(2) (exemptions with respect to specified schools and circumstances), the provider would be required to be registered [s.76(1)]

■ A person who is disqualified from registration by regulations under s.75 must not:

- Provide early years or later years provision to which s.76 applies, or
- Be directly concerned in the management of early years or later years provision to which s.76 applies [s.76(2)]

■ No person may employ, in connection with the provision of early years or later years provision to which this section applies, a person who is disqualified from registration by regulations under s.75 [s.76(3)].

■ A person who contravenes s.76(2) or s.76(3) commits an offence [s.76(4)].

■ A person who contravenes s.76(2) is **not guilty** of an offence under s.76(4) if:

- S/he is disqualified from registration by virtue only of regulations under s.75(4), and
- S/he proves that s/he did not know, and had no reasonable grounds for believing, that s/he was living in the same household as a person who was disqualified from registration, or in a household in which such a person was employed [s.75(5)]

■ A person who contravenes s.76 (3) is not guilty of an offence under s.76 (4) if s/he proves that s/he did not know, and had no reasonable grounds for believing, that the person whom s/he was employing was disqualified from registration [s.76(6)].

■ A person guilty of an offence under subsection (4) is liable on summary conviction to imprisonment for a maximum 51 weeks, a fine not exceeding level 5 on the standard scale, or both [s.76(7)].

NB. In relation to an offence committed before the commencement of s.281 (5) Criminal Justice Act 2003 (alteration of penalties for summary offences), the reference above to 51 weeks is to be read as a reference to 6 months [s.76 (8)].

Current Disqualification Arrangements

■ S.102 amended the Children Act 1989 provisions for disqualification for registration (para.4 Sch 9A) by adding to the existing criteria:

- Grounds relating to health
- 'Cautions' given in relation to the offences set out in the Day Care and Child Minding (Disqualification) (England) Regulations 2005 (including reprimands or warnings as per s.65 Crime and Disorder Act 1998)

■ Thus the Day Care and Child Minding (Disqualification) (England) (Amendment) Regulations 2007 (2007 S.I. 197) – in force from 28th February 2007 – sets out the current categories of persons disqualified from:

- Registration in England as child minders or day care providers for under 8s
- Employment in connection with day care provision
- Direct concern in the management of any day care provision

Rights of Entry

Powers of Entry [s.77]

■ A person authorised for this purpose by the Chief Inspector may at any reasonable time enter any premises in England if s/he has reasonable cause to believe that early years provision or later years provision is being provided on the premises in breach of s.33(1), 34(1), 52(1) or 53(1) [s.77(1)].

■ A person authorised for this purpose by the Chief Inspector may at any reasonable time enter any premises in England on which early years provision or later years provision in respect of which a person is registered under Part 3 is being provided:

- For the purpose of conducting an inspection under ss.49 or 60, or
- For the purpose of determining whether any conditions or requirements imposed by or under Part 3 are being complied with [s.77(2)]

■ Authorisation under s.77(1) or (2) may be given:

- For a particular occasion or period
- Subject to conditions [s.77(3)]

■ A person entering premises under s.77 may, subject to any conditions imposed as immediately above:

- Inspect the premises
- Inspect, and take copies of any records kept by the person providing the childcare, and any

other documents containing information relating to that provision

- Seize and remove any document or other material or thing found there which s/he has reasonable grounds to believe may be evidence of a failure to comply with any condition or requirement imposed by or under Part 3
- Take measurements and photographs or make recordings
- Inspect any children being cared for there, and the arrangements made for their welfare
- Interview in private the childcare provider
- Interview in private any person caring for children, or living or working, on the premises who consents to be interviewed [s.77(4)]

■ A person entering premises under s.77 may (subject to any conditions imposed as per s.73(3) require any person to afford her/him such facilities and assistance with respect to matters within the person's control as are necessary to enable her/him to exercise her/his powers under s.77 [s.77(5)].

■ A person exercising any power conferred by s.77 must, if so required, produce a duly authenticated document showing her/his authority to do so [s.77(7)].

■ A person commits an offence if s/he intentionally obstructs a person exercising any power under s.77 [s.77 (8)].

- A person guilty of an offence under s.77 (8) is liable on summary conviction to a fine not exceeding level 4 on the standard scale [s.77 (9)].

  NB. In s77 'document' and 'records' each include information recorded in any form [s.77 (10].

Requirement for Consent to Entry [s.78]

- S.78 applies where a person ('the authorised person') proposes to enter domestic premises in pursuance of:

  - Provision made by virtue of s.42(1) and (4) in a learning and development order specifying assessment arrangements in relation to early years provision, or
  - A power of entry conferred by s.77(2) [s.78(1)]

- The authorised person may not enter the premises without the consent of an adult occupier of the premises in circumstances where the authorised person has reasonable cause to believe that the premises:

  - Are not the home of the person providing the early years or later years provision, or
  - Are the home of a child for whom the early years or later years provision is provided [s.78(2)]

- S.78(2) does not prevent the imposition under ss.38, 58 or 66 of a condition requiring a registered person to secure that the occupier of any premises on which the registered person provides early years provision or later years provision gives any consent required by s.78(2)[s.78(3)].

NB. In s.78 a 'learning and development order' means an order under s.39 (1)(a) and an 'occupier' does not include the person providing the early years or later years provision [s.78(4)].

Power of Constable to Assist in Exercise of Powers of Entry [s.79]

■ A person authorised for the purpose of s.77 (1) or s.77 (2) may apply to a court for a warrant under s.79.

■ The court may issue a warrant authorising any constable to assist that person in the exercise of the power, using reasonable force if necessary, **if** it appears to the court that the authorised person:

- Has attempted to exercise a power conferred on her/him by s.77 but has been prevented from doing so, or
- Is likely to be prevented from exercising any such power [s.79(2)]

■ A warrant issued under s.79 must be addressed to, and executed by, a constable [s.79 (3)].

NB. Subject to any provision of Schedule 11 of the Children Act 1989 proceedings under s.79 may be brought in the High Court, a county court or a magistrates' court [s.79(4);(5)].

Reports & Information

Combined Reports [s.80]

■ This section applies if, following inspections under Part 3 of early years or later years provision, the Chief Inspector is required to make:

- More than one report under s.50(1) or determines to make more than one report under s.61(1), or
- One or more reports under s.50(1) and determines to make one or more reports under s.61(1) [s.80(1)]

■ If the Chief Inspector considers it appropriate, s/he may:

- Combine any two or more of those reports in a single document ('a combined report'), and
- To such extent as s/he considers appropriate, combine the substantive reports [s.80(2)]

■ If the Chief Inspector combines reports under s.80, the powers and

■ duties which apply in relation to each report by virtue of ss.50(2) or 61(2) are to be read as applying instead to the combined report [s.80(3)].

Information to be Included in Annual Reports [s.81]

■ The annual reports of the Chief Inspector required by s.3(a) Education Act 2005 to be made to the

Secretary of State must include an account of the exercise of the Chief Inspector's functions under Part 3 in relation to early years provision and later years provision [s.81(1)].

Supply of Information to Chief Inspector [s.82]

- The Chief Inspector may at any time require any person registered under Part 3 to provide her/him with any information connected with the person's activities as an early years provider or later years provider which the Chief Inspector considers it necessary to have for the purposes of her/his functions under Part 3 [s.82(1)].

Supply of Information to Her Majesty's Revenue & Customs & Local Authorities [s.83]

- The Chief Inspector must provide prescribed information to Her Majesty's Revenue and Customs, and the relevant local authority, if s/he takes any of the following steps under Part 3:

  - Grants a person's application for registration
  - Gives notice of her/his intention to cancel a person's registration
  - Cancels a person's registration
  - Suspends a person's registration
  - Removes a person from the register at that person's request [s.83(1)]

- The Chief Inspector must also provide prescribed information to Her Majesty's Revenue and Customs, and the relevant local authority, if an order is made under s.72(2) [s.83(2)].

- The information which may be prescribed for the purposes s.83 is:

  - In the case of information to be provided to Her Majesty's Revenue and Customs, information which Her Majesty's Revenue and Customs may require for the purposes of their functions in relation to tax credits
  - In the case of information to be provided to the relevant local authority, information which would assist the local authority in the discharge of their functions under section 12 (running an information service) [s.83 (3)]

NB. In s.83, 'relevant local authority' means the English local authority for the area in which the person provides/has provided) early or later years provision in respect of which s/he is/was registered [s.83(4)].

Disclosure of Information for Certain Purposes [s.84]

- The Chief Inspector may arrange for prescribed information held by her/him in relation to registered persons to be made available for the purpose of:

  - Assisting parents or prospective parents in choosing an early years or later years provider, or
  - Protecting children from harm or neglect [s.84(1)]

■ The information may be made available in such manner and to such persons as the Chief Inspector considers appropriate [s.84 (2)].

■ Regulations may require the Chief Inspector to provide prescribed information held by her/him in relation to persons registered under Part 3 to prescribed persons for either of the purposes mentioned in s.83(1) [s.83(3)].

Offences & Criminal Proceedings

Offence of Making False or Misleading Statement [s.85]

- A person commits an offence if, in an application for registration s/he knowingly makes a statement which is false or misleading in a material particular [s.85(1)].

- A person guilty of an offence under s.85(1) is liable on summary conviction to a fine not exceeding level 5 on the standard scale [s.85(2)].

Time Limit for Proceedings [s.86]

- Proceedings for an offence under Part 3 or regulations made under it may be brought within a period of 6 months from the date on which evidence sufficient in the opinion of the prosecutor to warrant the proceedings comes to her/his knowledge [s.86(1)].

- No such proceedings may be brought by virtue of s.86 (1) more than 3 years after the commission of the offence [s.86(2)].

Offences by Corporate Bodies and Unincorporated Associations [s.87; 88]

- If an offence is proved to have been committed with the consent or connivance of, or to be attributable to any neglect on the part of, any director, manager or other similar officer of an **incorporated body,** or any person who was purporting to act in any such capacity, s/he (as well as the body corporate) is guilty of the offence and liable to be proceeded against and punished accordingly [s.87 (2)].

■ Proceedings for an offence Part 3 alleged to have been committed by an **unincorporated association** must be brought in the name of the association (and not in the name of any of its members) [s.88(1)].

■ For the purpose of any such proceedings, rules of court relating to the service of documents are to have effect as if the association were a body corporate [s.88(3)].

■ In proceedings for an offence under Part 3 brought against an unincorporated association, s.33 of the Criminal Justice Act 1925 and Schedule 3 Magistrates' Courts Act 1980 (procedure) apply as they do in relation to a body corporate [s.88(3)] i.e. the association is treated as if it were an incorporated body.

■ A fine imposed on an unincorporated association on its conviction of an offence under Part 3 is to be paid out of the funds of the association [s.88(4)].

■ The officer or member, as well as the association is guilty of the offence and liable to be proceeded against and punished accordingly, **if** an offence under Part 3 by an unincorporated association is shown:

- To have been committed with the consent or connivance of an officer of the association or a member of its governing body, or
- To be attributable to any neglect on the part of such an officer or member [s.88(5)]

Miscellaneous & Interpretation

Fees [s.89]

- Regulations may require registered persons to pay to the Chief Inspector at or by prescribed times, fees of the prescribed amounts in respect of the discharge by the Chief Inspector of her/his functions under Part 3 [s.89(1)].

- The above regulations may prescribe circumstances in which:

  - The amount of a fee payable under the regulations may be varied in accordance with the regulations
  - A fee payable under the regulations may be waived [s.89 (2)].

The Day Care and Child Minding (Registration Fees) (England) (Amendment) Regulations 2006

- The above regulations amended (with effect from October 2006) the Day Care and Child Minding (Registration Fees) (England) Regulations 2005.

- Day care providers and child minders looking after children under the age of 8 are currently required to register under Part 10A of the Children Act 1989. The Regulations increased the fee for an application for registration as a day care provider from £121 to £150 if the provider provides at least 4 hours care a day and from £14 to £18 if s/he provides less than 4 hours a day.

- The fee for an application for registration as a child minder was increased from £14 to £18.

- The annual fee payable by registered day care providers was increased from £94 to £120 (if at least 4 hours care a day is provided) and from £11 to £14 when less than 4 hours care is provided.

- The annual fee payable by registered child minders was increased from £11 to £14.

Cases where Consent to Disclosure Withheld [s.90]

- S.90 applies where the Chief Inspector:

  - Is determining, for the purpose of deciding whether to grant an application for registration, whether the prescribed requirements for registration are satisfied and are likely to be continued to be satisfied, or
  - Is determining, for the purpose of deciding whether to cancel the registration of any person under s.68(2)(a), whether the prescribed requirements for registration have ceased, or will cease, to be satisfied [s.90(1)]

- The Chief Inspector may, if regulations so provide and s/he thinks it appropriate to do so, treat the prescribed requirements for registration as not being satisfied or (as the case may be) as having ceased to be satisfied if for the purpose of her/his determination:

- The Chief Inspector has requested a person ('A')
  to consent to the disclosure by another person
  ('B') to the Chief Inspector of information which
  relates to A, is held by B, and is of a prescribed
  description, and
- 'A' does not give her/his consent or withdraws
  consent after giving it [s.90(2)]

Co-operation between Authorities [s.91]

■ If it appears to the Chief Inspector that any English
local authority could, by taking any specified action,
help in the exercise of any of her/his functions
under Part 3, s/he may request the help of the
authority, specifying the action in question [s.91(1)].

■ An authority whose help is requested must comply
with the request if it is compatible with its own
statutory and other duties and does not unduly
prejudice the discharge of any of its functions
[s.91(2)].

Combined Certificates of Registration [s.92]

■ If the Chief Inspector is required by virtue of Part 3
to issue more than one certificate of registration to a
person and s/he considers it appropriate, s/he may
combine any two or more of those certificates in a
single certificate (a combined certificate)
[s.92(1);(2)].

■ A combined certificate of registration must contain
prescribed information about prescribed matters.

- If there is a change of circumstances which requires the amendment of a combined certificate of registration, the Chief Inspector must give the registered person an amended combined certificate.

- If the Chief Inspector is satisfied that a combined certificate of registration has been lost or destroyed, the Chief Inspector must give the registered person a copy, on payment by that person of any prescribed fee [s.95(5)].

Notices [s.93]

- In relation to notices to registered providers or applicants (decisions to refuse registration, impose conditions or cancel registration) and notices given by applicants and registered persons (giving notice they wish to be registered on another register or part of a register, wish to be removed from a register or do not intend to object to the taking of a step by the Chief Inspector under s.73) the notice may be given to the person in question:

  - By delivering it to her/him
  - By sending it by post, or
  - Subject to s.93 (3), by transmitting it electronically [s.93(1);(2)]

- **If** the notice is transmitted electronically, it is to be treated as 'given' **only**:

  - (If the person required or authorised to give the notice is the Chief Inspector) the person to whom the notice is required or authorised to be given has indicated to the Chief Inspector a willingness to receive notices transmitted electronically and provided an address suitable for that purpose, and the notice is sent to the address provided by her/him

- (If the person required or authorised to give the notice is not the Chief Inspector), the notice is transmitted in such manner as the Chief Inspector may require [s.93(3)-(5)]

NB. An indication given for the above purpose may be given generally for the purposes of notices required or authorised to be given by the Chief Inspector under Part 3 or may be limited to notices of a particular description [s.93(6)].

■ A requirement imposed by the Chief Inspector under s.93(5) must be published in such manner as the Chief Inspector thinks appropriate for the purpose of bringing it to the attention of persons who are likely to be affected by it [s.93(7)].

■ In relation to the taking of a s.73 step to impose a new condition on a person's registration or to vary or remove any condition imposed, the notification to be given to the Chief Inspector as per s.73(4) or (9) may be given orally to a person authorised by the Chief Inspector to receive it, as well as by any of the methods mentioned in s.93(2) above [s.93(7)].

Power to Amend Part 3: Applications in Respect of Multiple Premises [s.94]

■ The Secretary of State may by order amend Part 3 so as to enable an application for registration under s.36(1), s.55(1) or s.63(1) to be made in respect of more than one set of premises, and make further consequential amendments [s.94].

Employees Not to Be Regarded as Providing Childcare [s.97]

■ For the purposes of Part 3, if an employee is employed to care for a child by a person who provides early years or later years provision for her/him, the employee is **not** to be regarded as providing early years (or as the case may be later years) provision by virtue of anything done in the course of that employment [s.97.

NB. In such cases, the employer is under an obligation as the early or later years provider to ensure that the provision meets legal requirements(e.g. learning and development requirements) and is also obliged to ensure that they do not employ any disqualified person [s.97(1);(2)].

Part 4: Miscellaneous & General

Provision of Information About Children – England & Wales

■ Regulations may make provision, in relation to **England,** requiring persons registered as early years providers and school-based providers exempted from registration requirement by s.34(2) to provide such individual child information as may be prescribed, to:

- The Secretary of State, and
- Any prescribed person (in practice local authorities) [s.99(1);(2)]

■ Where such a prescribed person receives information by virtue of s.99(1), the Secretary of State may require that person to provide any such information to:

- The Secretary of State, or
- Any prescribed person [s.99(3)]

■ The Secretary of State may provide any individual child information to any:

- Information collator
- Prescribed person, or
- Person falling within a prescribed category [s.99(4)]

■ Any information collator may:

- Provide any individual child information to the Secretary of State, or to any other information collator, and

- May at such times as the Secretary of State may determine or in prescribed circumstances provide such individual child information as may be prescribed to any prescribed person, or to any person falling within a prescribed category [s.99(5)]

■ Any person holding any individual child information (other than the Secretary of State or an information collator) may provide that information to:

- The Secretary of State,
- Any information collator, or
- Any prescribed person [s.99(6)]

■ No information received under or by virtue of s.99 can be published in any form which includes the name of the child or children to whom it relates [s.99(7)].

■ Regulations may make provision, in relation to **Wales**, requiring a person who is registered under Part 10A of the Children Act 1989 to provide child minding or day care, and a person who provides funded nursery education, such individual child information as may be prescribed to:

- The Assembly, and
- Any prescribed person [s.101(1);(2)]

■ Where any such prescribed person receives information by virtue of s.101(1), the Assembly may require that person to provide any such information to:

- The Assembly, or
- Any prescribed person [s.101(3)]

■ The Assembly may provide any individual child information to any:

- Information collator
- Prescribed person, or
- Person falling within a prescribed category [s.101(4)]

■ Any information collator may:

- Provide any individual child information to the Assembly, or to any other information collator, and
- May at such times as the Assembly may determine or in prescribed circumstances provide such individual child information as may be prescribed to any prescribed person, or to any person falling within a prescribed category [s.101(5)]

■ Any person holding any individual child information (other than the Assembly or an information collator) may provide that information to:

- The Assembly
- Any information collator, or
- Any prescribed person [s.101 (6)].

■ No information received under or by virtue of this section can be published in any form which includes the name of the child or children to whom it relates [s.101(7)].

Appendix 1: Implementation Schedule

- The following came into force on 20th December 2006:

  - S.1,s.11, s.12 and s.13 for the purpose of making regulations
  - S.18 (meaning of childcare), s.19 (meaning of young child), s.20 (meaning of early years provision) and s.21 (interpretation of Part 1)
  - S.39 (Early Years Foundation Stage), s.41 (learning and development requirements), s.42 (further provisions about assessment arrangements), s.43 (welfare requirements), s.44 (instruments specifying learning and development or welfare requirements) s.45(procedure for making certain orders) and s.46 (power to enable exemptions to be conferred)
  - Ss.62,63,64,69,74,83,84,90,92,96 and 99 for the pupose of making regulations
  - S.71 (termination of voluntary registration on expiry of prescribed period), s.75 (disqualification from registration), s.89 (fees), s.98 (interpretation of Part 3) and s.100 (provision of information about young children: transitory provision)
  - S.102 (disqualification for registration under Children Act 1989) in relation to England

■ Other sections are due to come into force as follows:

- S.11 (duty to assess childcare provision) April 2007
- S.8 (power of local authority in relation to provision of childcare), s.9 (arrangements between local authority and childcare providers), s.10 (charges where local authority provide childcare), s.13 (duty to provide information, advice and training to childcare providers) – October 2007
- S.6 (duty to secure sufficient childcare for working parents) April 2008
- S.7 (duty to secure prescribed early years provision free of charge) September 2008

Appendix 2: Source Material

- Childcare Act 2006

- The Childcare Act (Local Authority Targets) Regulations 2007 [draft version]

- The Childcare (Provision of Information) Regulations 2006 [draft version]

- The Childcare Act 2006 (Commencement No.1) Order 2006 S.I. 3360

- Statutory Guidance on section 12 – the Duty to Provide Information, Advice and Assistance

- The Day Care and Child Minding (Disqualification) (England) (Amendment) Regulations 2007 S.I. 197

- The Day Care and Child Minding (Registration Fees) (England) (Amendment) Regulations 2006

- Every Child Matters Green Paper 2003

- *Choice for parents – the best start for children: a ten year strategy for childcare* – HM Treasury 2004

- *Childcare is for Children* Welsh Assembly 2005

Appendix 3: CAE Publications

- Personal Guides:

  - Children Act 1989 in the Context of the Human Rights Act 1998
  - Children Act 2004
  - Child Protection
  - Residential Care of Children
  - Fostering
  - 'How Old Do I Have To Be...?' (simple guide to the rights and responsibilities of 0 – 21 year olds)
  - Domestic Violence – (Part IV Family Law Act 1996 & Protection from Harassment Act 1997)
  - Crime and Disorder Act 1998
  - Sexual Offences Act 2003
  - Anti Social Behaviour
  - Childcare Act 2006

Available from: Children Act Enterprises Ltd
103 Mayfield Road South Croydon Surrey CR2 0BH
tel: 020 8651 0554 fax: 020 8405 8483
email: childact@dial.pipex.com

www.caeuk.org

Discounts for orders of 50 or more of any one title